A CONTEMPORARY CELTIC PRAYER BOOK

William John Fitzgerald

Foreword by Joyce Rupp

ACTA
PUBLICATIONS

A Contemporary Celtic Prayer Book
by William John Fitzgerald

Passages from the New Testament and the Psalms from *The Inclusive New Testament* and *The Inclusive Psalms,* 1997, are used with permission of Priests for Equality, P.O. Box 5243, W. Hyattsville, MD.

Passages from the Old Testament from *People's Companion to the Breviary, Volume II, Revised and Expanded Edition of the New Companion to the Breviary with Seasonal Supplement,* 1997, used with permission of the Carmelite Monastery, 2500 Cold Spring Road, Indianapolis, IN 46222, 1997.

Selections from *Carmina Gadelica: Hymns and Incantations* (Gaelic title, *Ortha nan Gaidheal*), edited by Alexander Carmichael, 1941, are used with permission of the Scottish Academic Press, 56 Hanover Street, Edinburgh, Scotland, EH22DX.

Edited by Kass Dotterweich
Cover art by Tom A. Wright
Typesetting by Garrison Publications

Copyright © 1998 by William John Fitzgerald

Published by   ACTA Publications
                Assisting Christians To Act
                4848 N. Clark Street
                Chicago, IL 60640
                773-271-1030

Library of Congress catalog card number: 98-73095
ISBN: 0-87946-189-6
Printed in the United States of America
05 04 03 02 01 5 4 3 2

CONTENTS

PART I: A CELTIC LITURGY OF THE HOURS

PART II: CELTIC BLESSINGS, PRAYERS, AND RITUALS

In memory of Father Larry Dorsey,
my Celtic anam cara

September 18, 1933–Saint Patrick's Eve, 1998

He has climbed Croagh Patrick and now
sees farther than any of us can dream.

Acknowledgments

Special thanks to the Trustees of the Scottish Academic Press for permission to use passages from *Carmina Gadelica;* to Priests for Equality for permission to use their new inclusive language translation of the Psalms and New Testament; to the Carmelite Sisters of Cold Spring Road, Indianapolis, Indiana, for permission to use their inclusive language translations from the Old Testament; to Father Bill Healy for his support and encouragement; to Father Alan Malone, native son of Galway, for the many resources he supplied; to Robert Reilly, mentor and author of *Red Hugh, Prince of Donegal* and other Irish books, for his helpful suggestions; and to Mary Glass of Wicklow and Dolores Whelan of Dundalk for a journey to the soul of Ireland. Finally, my appreciation to Joyce Rupp for contributing the Foreword to this book.

FOREWORD

I can still see the small forest of healthy green pines along
the Black River in northern Ireland. The profound emotion that these trees stirred in me is strongly wedded to my
memory. All week long, as I walked in the forest, touched
the branches, leaned against the trunks of trees, and lay on
the soft ground of pine needles, I felt a deep wave of
intense emotion while a great peace settled in my soul. I
stood silently amid the trees, taking in deep breaths of an
air that seemed both earthly and eternal. I hummed. I
sang. Each time I walked into that sacred place, I felt as
though I never wanted to leave. Something in that dark,
earthy, moist, forest felt like "home" to me. Something in
that quiet realm spoke to me of an energy dwelling in the
land long before I was there, an energy thick with life and
vitality.

At that time I knew little about Celtic history and
spirituality. Four years later, when I started a yearlong
study of Celtic wisdom, I found myself going back in
memory to that week of walking in the forest along the
river. As I recalled my days in the pine forest, everything in
me said "yes" to what I was learning about this valuable
spiritual tradition. My daily walk in the forest had drawn
me to a mystical sense of the Celtic spirit, and that experience was confirmed through my studies. The reading,
teaching, ritual, and many conversations I had regarding
the beauty and power of Celtic spirituality further con-
vinced me of the vibrancy of this heritage.

It is my hope that the current interest in Celtic
spirituality and wisdom is more than a passing fad, for

there is such richness and beauty in the Celtic legacy. I marvel at how closely attuned the Celts were to creation and how readily they recognized the presence of God in every piece and pattern of their lives. I long for the depth and quality of this ancestral wealth to be shared with all who search for a way to live with deeper meaning and inspiration.

What a joy it is to be introduced to William Fitzgerald's wonderful prayer book. He takes the Celts' intimate and appreciative relationship with nature and brings it alive in a way that draws us, as well, to the power of creation. He invites us into life and urges us to see that the "divine allurement fills the universe." His contemporary prayers reflect the enticing and captivating energy that was part of the Celtic people's faith.

Like the Celts of long ago who took the many threads of their ordinary, daily lives and wove prayer into their rising, working, sleeping, dreaming, so William Fitzgerald interlaces the commonness of our lives with the imminent presence of divinity. In our busy world where we still tend to keep our daily life and our life with God in separate corners, it is heartening to see how this author honors the Celtic tradition. He intertwines the ordinary and the exalted by giving us prayers that resound out of our daily life experiences. His blessings for home and child, meals and journey, soul friends and the dying are just a few of the many prayers he spins out of the Celtic era and into our lives.

By suggesting that we use three key moments of the day as centerpieces for these prayers, William Fitzgerald gives us a built-in spiritual discipline. His "Celtic Liturgy of the Hours" is a way to integrate every aspect of our life with our relationship to the divine. The sacredness of "the hours" creates an ongoing call to be intentional about our intimate bond with the Indwelling One. These morsels of communication with God remind us that we are not disparate, separate spiritual creatures. Rather, all we are and all we do constitute the warp and woof of our spiritual path.

Celtic prayers began as songs and poems that were shared orally over a long period of time. Because of this, they have a repetitive, lyrical quality about them. One can imagine these prayers being sung not once but repeatedly, as the cows were milked and the bread was baked. Since he is of Celtic heritage himself, it is easy to hear the author's poetic spirit in these lovely, rhythmical, and free-spirited prayers. Among these creative patterns are litanies, encircling prayers, and breastplate (protective) prayers. Celtic Christians held Christ and the cross in a central place in their spirituality. The Trinity is one of the many "threes" which formed a key structure for their prayers, along with a great devotion to Mary and the saints. All of these Celtic elements give unique flavor to the prayers presented in this book.

Whether or not you ever step upon the green land of a Celtic country, whether or not you ever slip into an ethereal forest, whether or not you ever gaze upon a Celtic sea–you can still find inspiration and connection with the earthy, mystical power of the Celtic faith. I think you will find these prayers leading you to a place within yourself that sings with the spirituality of the Celtic ancestors. I hope these creative prayers enliven your enthusiasm for the great adventure of life and that they will assure you of the nearness of your God.

Joyce Rupp

INTRODUCTION

In the Kilmalkedar churchyard, on a mountain in Kerry in western Ireland, there stands an ancient sundial–perhaps a thousand years old–carved into the face of a standing stone. On the surface of the sundial, there are marks for the daytime canonical hours–the times each day when monks, nuns, and laypeople would chant the Liturgy of the Hours.

A Contemporary Celtic Prayer Book attempts to capture the flavor of Celtic spirituality for today's busy Christians, who may be able to use the sensibilities of the people of the lands of Ireland, Scotland, Wales, and Brittany to make sense of their hectic lives. This prayer book is meant to be a prayer companion that can be carried in a purse or briefcase and used daily–or whenever the Spirit moves one to pray.

When I say that these prayers are "Celtic," I mean that they capture the flavors and characteristics of prayer, devotion, and worldview that have come down to us from the golden age of the Celts, approximately 500-700 A.D., when Ireland became known as the "land of saints and scholars." This spirituality had its roots in pre-Christian Celtic experience, not the Roman empire. Patrick and the other Christian missionaries took what was compatible in pagan usage and planted the seeds of the gospel in this rich soil. What bloomed was a unique way of looking at the world and communicating with the divine that we now call "Celtic."

Part I, "A Celtic Liturgy of the Hours," provides three prayer breaks–morning, midday, and night–in a modified version of the Liturgy of the Hours. By following these prayer times with this book, you can be in touch with a prayer routine that is older than the Kilmalkedar sundial and yet is still honored in the official daily prayer of the Church. Merely pick three times a day—one in the morning, one at midday, and one in the evening—when you regularly turn your thoughts to God.

At the very beginning of Part I, you will find Daily Prayers (page 11): the Magnificat, the Our Father, and the Hail Mary. These prayers are positioned for convenient reference, so you can turn to them when you are directed (indicated by the names of the prayers in bold).

Morning Prayer, or the Hour of Lauds, offers two prayer options after the Morning Offering: Option A and Option B. The first option applies to people going to work. Persons staying at home may prefer the second option, which is designed more for their needs.

The Noon Prayer is called the Hour of Nones and Angelus, to tie it to both the Liturgy of the Hours and the other popular devotion of reciting the Angelus at midday. (Many monastic houses today have combined the hours of Sext and Nones into one midday prayer.)

In each Night Prayer, or Hour of Compline, I suggest meditating on a famous Celtic locale and offer several choices—all actual places. Feel free, however, to substitute a favorite place in your own current or native land. Since many people go out on Friday nights, the Night Prayer on Friday is designed to be prayed early and thus is called Sunset Prayer, or the Hour of Vespers.

At the end of Part I, you will find lists of Alternate Readings (page 90), which offer Alternate Psalms for

Morning Prayer, Alternate Canticles for Morning Prayer, and Alternate Readings for Night Prayer. You will also find a list identifying the specific locations of those places mentioned in the Meditative Moment in a Celtic Land section of each day's Night Prayer (page 98).

Part II, "Celtic Blessings, Prayers, and Rituals," offers a variety of blessings and prayers from original Celtic sources, as well as new blessings and prayers fashioned in the Celtic tradition. (My McCarthy, Garrahan, and O'Byrne ancestors have passed on this tradition to me pretty much intact, as did the Fitzgeralds, who came late to Ireland but ended up being as Irish as the others.) This section includes: blessings for friends, family, and daily occasions; prayers to Celtic saints and for special intentions; prayers for the "shadow times" of sickness, the "thin times" of death and mourning, the "moontimes" of love and romance; and prayers and rituals for the cycles of the earth and the Church. How and when to use these prayers, blessings, and rituals depend on your own needs and whims.

Because particular words, phrases, and names may not be familiar, I provide a Glossary for your convenience (page 137). In general, however, the language in this prayer book should be understandable by all. Wherever possible– unless ancient sources made it impossible–I use inclusive language. (I think that strong Celtic women like Saint Brigid, Mother Catherine McAuley, Saint Ita, Queen Margaret of Scotland, and even Grace O'Malley would have approved.)

A Contemporary Celtic Prayer Book is a new prayer resource based on a very old way of prayer. Like the

sundial in Kilmalkedar, may it point the way to God for
many and for many years. And as the Celts would say,
"May God be with your days!"

PART I

A CELTIC LITURGY OF THE HOURS

DAILY PRAYERS

The Magnificat

My soul proclaims your greatness, O God,
and my spirit rejoices in you, my Savior.
For you have looked with favor
upon your lowly servant,
and from this day forward
all generations will call me blessed.
For you, the Almighty, have done great things for me,
and holy is your Name.
Your mercy reaches from age to age
for those who fear you.
You have shown strength with your arm,
you have scattered the proud in their conceit,
you have deposed the mighty from their thrones
and raised the lowly to high places.
You have filled the hungry with good things,
while you have sent the rich away empty.
You have come to the aid of Israel your servant,
mindful of your mercy—
the promise you made to our ancestors—
to Sarah and Abraham
and their descendants forever.

Luke 1:46-55

The Our Father

Our Father,
Who art in heaven,
Hallowed be thy name.
Thy kingdom come,
Thy will be done,
On earth
As it is in heaven.
Give us this day
Our daily bread,
And forgive us our trespasses
As we forgive those who trespass against us.
Lead us not into temptation,
But deliver us from evil. Amen.

The Hail Mary

Hail, Mary, full of grace.
The Lord is with you.
Blessed are you among women,
And blessed is the fruit of your womb, Jesus.
Holy Mary, Mother of God,
Pray for us sinners,
Now and at the hour of our death. Amen.

SUNDAY

Celtic spirituality contains wonderful elements of joyful celebration. Kinship brings joy, whether it is within the tribe or family or with all the other creatures in the great circle of living beings. The Celts, pagan or Christian, had a deep sense of enchantment with the beauty and mystery all around them. Celtic prayer very often starts with taking pleasure in original *blessings* more than lamenting original *sin.* In doing so, it communicates a primal joy. The tradition of Sabbath rest and peace, and the slower pace of life that has disappeared in most modern countries, still lingers in Celtic lands.

Morning Prayer

Opening Prayer: O God, come to our assistance. O God, make haste to help us. Glory to the One in Three as it was in the beginning, is now, and evermore shall be.

Hymn

I will raise the hearth-fire
As Mary would.
The encirclement of Bride and of Mary
On the fire, and on the floor,
And on the household all.

Who are they on the bare floor?
John and Peter and Paul.
Who are they by my bed?
The lovely Bride and her Fosterling.
Who are those watching over my sleep?
The fair loving Mary and her Lamb.
Who is that anear me?
The King of the sun, He himself it is.
Who is that at the back of my head?
The Son of Life without beginning, without time.

"KINDLING THE FIRE,"
Carmina Gadelica, Vol. I, p. 233

Canticle

All you works of God, praise our God.
Praise and exalt God above all forever.
All you angels, sing God's praise,
you heavens and waters above.
Sun and moon, and stars of heaven,
sing praise with the heavenly hosts.

Every shower and dew, praise our God.
Give praise all you winds.
Praise our God, you fire and heat,
cold and chill—dew and rain.
Frost and chill, praise our God.
Praise God, ice and snow.
Nights and days, sing hymns of praise,
light and darkness,
lightnings and clouds.

Let all the earth bless our God.
Praise and exalt God above all forever.
Let all that grows from the earth give praise
together with mountains and hills.
Give praise you springs,
you seas and rivers,
dolphins and all water creatures.
Let birds of the air,—
beasts wild and tame,
together with all living peoples,
praise and exalt God above all forever.

O Israel praise our God.
Praise and exalt God above all forever.

Give praise, you priests,
servants of the Most High,
spirits and souls of the just.
Holy ones of humble heart,
sing your hymns of praise.
Hananiah, Azariah, Mishael, praise our God.
Praise and exalt God above all forever.

Daniel 3:57-88

Meditative Moment: Look about and see (or imagine)
some of the creatures that daily raise their song or
chatter—birds, dolphins, squirrels. Perhaps take notice of a
tail-wagging dog, a purring cat. Each is praising God. As
the third Eucharistic Prayer of the Mass proclaims—all
creatures "rightly give God praise!"

Morning Offering: This morning, with all creation, I
join in joyful praise. I ask this blessing for the day: (add
your special intention for today).

Prayer at Rising (Option A)

God of all creatures,
Feathered, finned, or furred,
So dear to you,
Companions of the saints—
Colm Cille and the crane,
Pangor Ban, Kevin's raven,
Mochaoi's singing bird,
Patrick shapeshifted into a deer!

Let us soar like the crane
Beyond last week's din.

Let us purr like the kitten,
Curled up in Sunday rest.
Let us bond like the canines,
Finding kinship in our pack.
Let us be graced like the deer,
Bounding o'er life's pursuits.

Prayer at Rising (Option B)

Bless to me, O God,
    Each thing mine eye sees;
Bless to me, O God,
    Each sound mine ear hears;
Bless to me, O God,
    Each odour that goes to my nostrils;
Bless to me, O God,
    Each taste that goes to my lips;
    Each note that goes to my song,
    Each ray that guides my way,
    Each thing that I pursue,
    Each lure that tempts my will,
    The zeal that seeks my living soul,
The Three that seek my heart,
    The zeal that seeks my living soul,
The Three that seek my heart.

From Catherine Maclean, crofter, Naast, Gairloch,
Carmina Gadelica, Vol. III, p. 33

Midday Prayer

Let this Hour of Nones be an oasis
in the desert of Sunday busyness.

Scripture Reading

Meanwhile, Mary stood weeping beside the tomb. Even as she wept, she stooped to peer inside, and there she saw two angels in dazzling robes. One was seated at the head and the other at the foot of the place where Jesus' body had lain.

They asked her, "Why are you weeping?"

She answered them, "Because they have taken away my Rabbi, and I don't know where they have put the body."

No sooner had she said this than she turned around and caught sight of Jesus standing there, but she didn't know it was Jesus....

Jesus said to her, "Mary!"

John 20:11-14, 16

The Hail Mary...

Silence: Relax for a few moments and let go of the morning. Close your eyes and take several deep breaths until you feel your body relaxing.

Blessing of Self: I affirm and congratulate myself for...

Blessing the Sabbath

Blessed be Sunday.
Blessed be God's "shalom."
Blessed be the joy of kinship.
Blessed be the joy of friendship.
Blessed be the joy of breaking bread.
Blessed be the fruits of fertile earth.

Blessed be God for our kinship—
With all races and creeds,
And with all God's creatures.
God looks upon us all,
And it is all very good!

Blessing for Sunday Dinner

I am bathing my face
In the mild rays of the sun,
As Mary bathed Christ
In the rich milk of Egypt.

Sweetness be in my mouth,
Wisdom be in my speech,
The love the fair Mary gave her Son
Be in the heart of all flesh for me.

"THE LUSTRATION,"
Carmina Gadelica, Vol. I, p. 59, v. 1-2

NIGHT PRAYER

THE HOUR OF COMPLINE

Opening Prayer: O God, come to our assistance. O God, make haste to help us. Glory to the One in Three as it was in the beginning, is now, and evermore shall be.

Hymn

The charm placed by Brigit,
    Maiden of graces,
On the white daughter of the king,
    Gile-Mhin the beauteous.

The form of God is behind thee,
The form of Christ is before thee,
The stream of Spirit is through thee,
    To succour and aid thee.

The bloom of God is upon thee,
The bloom of Christ is upon thee,
The bloom of Spirit is upon thee,
    To bathe thee and make thee fair.

"CHARM OF GRACE,"
Carmina Gadelica, Vol. III, p. 217, v. 1-3

Meditative Moment in a Celtic Land

O God, let me quiet down so that I might ease into a new week and new challenges. (Close your eyes. Relax your body. Be peaceful. Imagine that you are sitting quietly in one of these scenes. Simply remain peaceful in the scene for several minutes.)

1. You are on a park bench beside a pleasant stream that meanders through a vibrant town. Under a nearby bridge, graceful white swans circle about.

2. You are in front of a waterfall that cascades over black rock. Growing at the base of the waterfall, where the water splashes with abandon, you see wild yellow gorse.

3. You sit on the porch of an elegant old manor and look out over the expanse of a beautifully mani-cured lawn. Nearby, you see several horses hitched to jaunting cars and munching out of feedbags. Across the lawn, at the hedgerow, you see several deer grazing contentedly.

4. You look out over a beautiful loch and gaze past a solitary lighthouse that keeps watch at the lake's side. You see majestic green mountains that rise and frame the scene.

Prayer for Healing, Renewal, and Reconciliation: If you recall this Sunday's readings, place yourself in the gospel scene and speak to Jesus there. Or picture Jesus offering living water to the woman at the well—and to you. Relax, and be served by Jesus (see John 4:26).

Prayer of Letting Go: Sweet Jesus and Mary, at the end of this weekend I am grateful for: (name one or more things).

The Our Father...

Prayer at the End of Day

I lie down tonight
With fair Mary and with her Son,
With pure-white Michael,
And with Bride beneath her mantle.

> *"SLEEP CONSECRATION,"*
> *Carmina Gadelica, Vol. I, p. 81, v. 1*

Intentions: At the end of this day, I pray for: (name the people and intentions you wish to pray for).

The Magnificat...

Blessing of the Night

May the good news of Jesus
Enter my sleep and guide me
Into the new week.

Prayer of Affirmation: Like a ship, I set sail toward a new week with Jesus at the wheel.

MONDAY

Celtic spirituality valued pilgrimages to holy places. On Monday, some of us make pilgrimages to "holy places" of work: to hearth-side or to commute. Some of us, confined or retired, continue our daily life pilgrimages on our walk with Jesus.

Morning Prayer

THE HOUR OF LAUDS

Opening Prayer: O God, come to our assistance. O God, make haste to help us. Glory to the One in Three as it was in the beginning, is now, and evermore shall be.

Hymn

I arise today
Through a mighty strength, the invocation of
   the Trinity,
Through belief in the threeness,
Through confession of the oneness
Of the Creator of Creation.

I arise today
Through the strength of Christ's birth with his baptism,
Through the strength of his crucifixion with his burial,
Through the strength of his resurrection with his
   ascension....

Saint Patrick's Breastplate

Psalm

Take note of my words, Adonai!
   Understand my sighs!
Listen to my cry for help, my Ruler, my God—
   for it is to you that I pray.
Adonai, every morning you hear my voice,

every morning I put my requests before you,
and I wait.
But I, because of your great love,
will enter your House;
I will worship in your holy Temple
in awe and reverence.
Because of my enemies, guide me in your justice;
make straight your way before me.
But let all who take refuge in you
be glad and rejoice forever.
Protect them,
so that those who love your Name
will rejoice in you.
As for the just, Adonai,
you surround them with the shield of your will.

Psalm 5:1-3, 7-8, 11-12

Meditative Moment: Pause to look at the clock, and think about the mystery of time. Every second, every minute, every hour, every day, is God's gift of time. It is a gift unearned, simply given.

Morning Offering: This morning, with all creation, I join in joyful praise. I ask this blessing for the day: (add your special intention for today).

Prayer at Rising (Option A)

God, bless our work this week,
From morning's waking
Till night's folding.
Bless our comings and goings,
The spinning of our labor and our lives.

May the ones we meet,
Even those with whom we compete,
Be the better for it.
God bless this week.
God bless this journey.
God bless the work.

Prayer at Rising (Option B)

Today, I begin the holy Seven,
Blessed by the holy Three.
Each day a blessing,
Each night a rest,
A dweller in a holy place.
Each day a page,
Each week a chapter
In the hand of God.

Midday Prayer

THE HOUR OF NONES AND ANGELUS

What good do my worries or fears accomplish?
I shall walk with Mary in joyful hope.

Scripture Reading

The angel went on to say to her, "Don't be afraid, Mary.
You have found favor with God."

Luke 1:30

The Hail Mary...

Silence: Relax for a few moments and let go of the
morning. Close your eyes and take several deep breaths
until you feel your body relaxing.

Blessing of Self: I affirm and congratulate myself for...

Lunch Blessing

Bless my Monday quests.
Bless the fruits of the earth.
Bless the hands of farmers.
Bless the hands of workers.
Bless the texture and colors of my food.
Bless those who gather.

Bless the breaking of bread.
Blessed Be! Blessed Be! Blessed Be!
Christ at every table,
Christ beside me,
Christ behind me,
Christ around me,
In the breaking of the bread.

NIGHT PRAYER

THE HOUR OF COMPLINE

Opening Prayer: O God, come to our assistance. O God, make haste to help us. Glory to the One in Three as it was in the beginning, is now, and evermore shall be.

Hymn

Bright Star of the West,
The first to shine,
Ode to origins divine.

Bright Star of the East,
Prepare the dawn,
You who led the Magi on.

Bright Star of the South,
O'er children's heads
Sprinkle stardust on their beds.

Bright Star of the North,
When time is done
Announce at last—all are one!

Meditative Moment in a Celtic Land

O God, let me calm down so that I might ease into the quiet of this night. (Close your eyes. Relax your body. Be peaceful. Imagine that you are sitting quietly in one of

these scenes. Simply remain peaceful in the scene for
several minutes.)

1. You sit on a green cliff at twilight. Below, you see
    the sandy seashore spreading like a crescent against
    the sea. You watch the surf as the sun departs.

2. You sit by the statue of Saint Brendan, whose arms
    extend westward to bless the sun as it disappears
    beyond the sea.

3. You stand on a cliff, facing north, and watch the sea
    below being swept by the power of the wind. You
    see the full moon casting a glow over dimpled hills
    and frothy waves.

4. You sit on a dock at end of day and look at the
    fishermen's boats securely moored, their blue net
    lines curled in tangled patterns on the dock. You
    hear nothing save the washing of the sea against the
    boats.

Prayer for Healing, Renewal, and Reconciliation: Picture
Jesus laying his hand upon your head and praying for
healing of what has bruised you today or for the hurt you
may have caused others (see Matthew 8:3).

Prayer of Letting Go: O God, let the cares of this day
flow away from me like the retreating ocean surf. At the
end of this day, I am grateful for: (name one or more
things).

The Our Father...

Prayer at the End of Day

All is gift!
The air I breathe,
The wind through the trees.
The breath of God breathes
In them and in me.
I breathe the air
That Jesus breathed.
I feel the wind
That Mary felt.
Every breath a thanks,
Every breeze a praise.

Intentions: At the end of this day, I pray for: (name the people and intentions you wish to pray for).

The Magnificat...

Blessing of the Night

Blessed be! Blessed be!
For my soul, too,
Magnifies God's presence!

Prayer of Affirmation: I am in God's care. I pull down the night over all my dreams.

TUESDAY

Celtic Spirituality had an intuitive wisdom for the connection of everyday life with the spirit world. Angels are near!
And the hearth-fire draws us near to all good spirits.

·

Morning Prayer

Opening Prayer: O God, come to our assistance. O God, make haste to help us. Glory to the One in Three as it was in the beginning, is now, and evermore shall be.

Hymn

> I arise today
> Through the strength of the love of Cherubim,
> In obedience of angels,
> In the service of archangels,...
>
> I arise today
> Through the strength of heaven:
> Light of sun,
> Radiance of moon,
> Splendor of fire,
> Speed of lightning,
> Swiftness of wind,
> Depth of sea,
> Stability of earth,
> Firmness of rock.

Saint Patrick's Breastplate

Psalm

You are tender and compassionate, Adonai—
    slow to anger, and always loving;
your indignation doesn't endure forever,
    and your anger lasts only for a short time.
You never treat us as our sins deserve;
    you don't repay us in kind for the injustices we do.
For as high as heaven is above the earth,
    so great is the love for those who revere you.
As far away as the east is from the west,
    that's how far you remove our sins from us!
As tenderly as parents treat their children,
    that's how tenderly you treat your
        worshipers, Adonai!
For you know what we are made of—
    you remember that we're nothing but dust.
We last no longer than grass,
    live no longer than a wildflower;
one gust of wind and we're gone,
    never to be seen again.
Yet your love lasts from age to age
    for those who revere you, Adonai,
as does your goodness to our children's children,
    and to those who keep your Covenant
    and remember to obey your precepts.
You have established your judgment seat in the
  heavens,
    and your reign extends over everything.

Bless Our God, you angels,
    you powers who do God's bidding,
    attentive to every word of command!

Bless Our God, you heavenly host,
    you faithful ones who enforce God's will!
Bless Our God, all creation,
    to the far reaches of God's reign!
Bless Adonai, my soul!

Psalm 103:8-22

Meditative Moment: Pause to look out the window,
reflect, and pray. Each morning the gift of light reappears.
Whether sunny or cloudy, blessed light returns to brighten
your path. Just as your ancestors lit the hearth at day's
beginning, God lights the sun to return and bless you.
Thanks be to God for kindling the light!

Morning Offering: This morning, with all creation, I join
in joyful praise. I ask this blessing for the day: (add your
special intention for today).

Prayer at Rising (Option A)

Rise energy—
Strength sustained,
Tuesday's work
For fingers trained.

Toil of our hands,
Work of our mind,
God's great grace
Is intertwined.

No worthy task,
Is entertained,

Till Spirit's gifts
Are full retained.

All our efforts
So maintained
By gifts of grace
Heaven is gained.

Bless the work.
Bless the day.
Come to aid us.
Angels stay!

Prayer at Rising (Option B)

The raven sings
Like a black-cowled friar
In ancient monastery choir.
On Patrick's mountain,
Violet heather–vested–prays,
And the gorse is golden
Like the edge of the dawn.

We once were wild geese
Above purple and gold.
I once was the heather
Guiding pilgrims home.
Rooted in earthiness,
Dark ages–eons of time,
Unfolds a future sublime.

This Tuesday's hours
More footsteps forward

Through sacred, gifted time.
With all creation
Singing sweet praise,
Holy! Holy! Holy!
Through all the days.

MIDDAY PRAYER

THE HOUR OF NONES AND ANGELUS

Angels, bearers of good tidings, awaken me to joy, to
divine presence whenever I experience what is good,
true, and beautiful. Let me take great joy in
recognizing beauty in the eyes of other good people.
It is there if I take time to really see.

Scripture Reading

The angel of God appeared to [the shepherds]. "...You
have nothing to fear! I come to proclaim good news to
you—news of a great joy to be shared by the whole
people."

Luke 2:9-10

The Hail Mary...

Silence: Relax for a few moments and let go of the
morning. Close your eyes and take several deep breaths
until you feel your body relaxing.

Blessing of Self: I affirm and congratulate myself for...

Lunch Blessing

Bless my Tuesday with moments of joy.
Bless the calloused hands of migrant workers.
Bless the flour-covered fingers of bakers.
Bless the texture and pleasing aromas of food.
Bless those who gather.
Bless the breaking of bread.
Blessed Be! Blessed Be! Blessed Be!
Christ at every table,
Christ beside me,
Christ behind me,
Christ around me,
In the breaking of the bread.

NIGHT PRAYER

THE HOUR OF COMPLINE

Opening Prayer: O God, come to our assistance. O God, make haste to help us. Glory to the One in Three as it was in the beginning, is now, and evermore shall be.

Hymn

The evening creeps in.
The shadows fall.
Now falls away the hours of toil.
Now falls away the hectic pace.
Now falls away the day's dissent.
Now falls away the discontent.
The evening envelops.
The darkness falls.
This day is past, let go regrets.
This night is now, enter in.
The hearth is lit; it casts a glow.
Kindle the heart from sparks below.

Meditative Moment in a Celtic Land

O God, let me calm down so that I might ease into the quiet of this night. (Close your eyes. Relax your body. Be peaceful. Imagine that you are sitting quietly in one of these scenes. Simply remain peaceful in the scene for several minutes.)

1. You watch a woman light the peat fire in her home's fireplace. It flickers and sends a glow upon the room.

2. You observe Saint Patrick upon a green hillock as he enkindles the great Easter fire that flames up into the night.

3. You sit on a whitewashed wall at twilight watching the twinkling stars shining above a white, thatch-roofed cottage. A puff of blue smoke winds up from the chimney.

4. You sit beside a restored stone church on a small island in the Irish Sea listening to the chant of monks greeting the night—much the same as their predecessors could have sung back in the sixth century.

Prayer for Healing, Renewal, and Reconciliation: Picture Jesus cooking fish over a charcoal fire, smiling and inviting you to come and eat (see John 21:9).

Prayer of Letting Go: O God, let the hearth fire burn away today's discontent. At the end of this day, I am grateful for: (name one or more things).

The Our Father...

Prayer at the End of Day

Through dark nights and ages,
Our ancestors lit their night fires.
They gathered around the circle
Telling their tales of the day.

O God, source of all holy fires,
Bless the story of my day.
Enlighten and warm my heart.
O God, send out your Spirit–
A tongue of fire above my head.
Let not the wick be quashed,
Nor the bruised reed trampled.

Intentions: At the end of this day, I pray for: (name the people and intentions you wish to pray for).

The Magnificat...

Blessing of the Night

Blessed Be! Blessed Be!
For my spirit, too, rejoices
In God my savior!

Prayer of Affirmation: I am in God's care. The wick shall not be quashed nor the bruised reed trampled.

WEDNESDAY

Celtic spirituality is attuned to the cycle of prayer. The Celts prayed around and around the Celtic cross. Wednesday is the center point of our week's holy work cycle.

Morning Prayer

Opening Prayer: O God, come to our assistance. O God, make haste to help us. Glory to the One in Three as it was in the beginning, is now, and evermore shall be.

Hymn

> I arise today
> Through God's strength to pilot me:
> God's might to uphold me,
> God's wisdom to guide me,
> God's eye to look before me,
> God's ear to hear me,
> God's word to speak for me,
> God's hand to guard me,
> God's way to lie before me,
> God's shield to protect me,
> God's host to save me
> From snares of devils,
> From temptations of vices,
> From everyone who shall wish me ill,
> Afar and anear,
> Alone and in multitude.

Saint Patrick's Breastplate

Canticle

Strike up the instruments,
a song to my God with timbrels,
chant to the Most High with cymbals.
Sing a new song,
exalt and acclaim God's name.

A new hymn I will sing to you.
O God, great are you and glorious,
wonderful in power and unsurpassable.

Let your every creature serve you;
for you spoke, and they were made,
you sent forth your spirit, and they were created;
no one can resist your word.

The mountains to their bases, and the seas, are shaken;
the rocks, like wax, melt before your glance.
But to those who fear you,
you are very merciful.

Judith 16:1, 13-15

Meditative Moment: Pause and gaze at pictures of loved ones. Consider these relationships more valuable than anything money can buy. Thank God for their influence on your life. Bless them today and every day, and pray for the rest and peace of deceased relatives and friends.

Morning Offering: This morning, with all creation, I join in joyful praise. I ask this blessing for the day: (add your special intention for today).

Prayer at Rising (Option A)

Midway in work-week's journey
Like a ship on its way through the sea,
I raise the sails of my spirit
And catch the wind of God's breath.

This week's story half logged,
Still time to adjust my course.
Saint Brendan, intrepid sailor,
Guide me till nightfall and harbor.

Prayer at Rising (Option B)

The middle is a good place to be.
The center around which life flows.
Bless my circle of friends.
Bless my circle of interests.
May I be encircled by love and peace.

Midday Prayer

Angel messengers assure me of God's care. If I
ask for a fish, I will not be given a stone. I ask
now for an oasis in this week half done.

Scripture Reading

The angel said to him, "Don't be frightened, Zechariah.
Your prayer has been heard."

Luke 1:13

The Hail Mary...

Silence: Relax for a few moments and let go of the
morning. Close your eyes and take several deep breaths
until you feel your body relaxing.

Blessing of Self: I affirm and congratulate myself for...

Lunch Blessing

Bless my Wednesday quest.
Bless the agile hands of fruit pickers.
Bless the creativity of cooks.
Bless the refreshing gift of clear water.
Bless those who gather.

Bless the breaking of bread.
Blessed Be! Blessed Be! Blessed Be!
Christ at every table,
Christ beside me,
Christ behind me,
Christ around me,
In the breaking of the bread.

NIGHT PRAYER

THE HOUR OF COMPLINE

Opening Prayer: O God, come to our assistance. O God, make haste to help us. Glory to the One in Three as it was in the beginning, is now, and evermore shall be.

Hymn

Celts pray round and round
The great cross in the circle.
Energy radiates out
From Christ—its center.

For us: "round and round"
Spins our wheel of fortune.
Wednesday's clock chimes—
Our work week is half done.

Office, farm, factory, home,
Our money being earned.
Is it really "filthy lucre"
Or rather—energy for good?

Money *doesn't* grow on trees.
Grant us work and just wages
To meet our daily needs
(And some extra for the poor).

Where else but in Ireland–
Once on its legal tender–a nun!
Catherine McAuley,
Merciful tender of the poor!

O God the great investor,
Loaner of time, talent, treasure,
Bless our work and earnings,
Make money energy for good.

Meditative Moment in a Celtic Land

O God, let me calm down so that I might ease into the
quiet of this night. (Close your eyes. Relax your body. Be
peaceful. Imagine that you are sitting quietly in one of
these scenes. Simply remain peaceful in the scene for
several minutes.)

1. You sit in a sun-drenched pasture that is hemmed in
   by a rock fence–rock set upon rock, with no mortar
   in between. In the middle of the pasture, looking
   back at you, stands a brown mare with a silver
   mane. Beside her is a spindly-legged colt, and
   beyond, sheep graze contentedly.

2. You sit on the edge of a lovely loch looking at the
   ruins of a medieval castle. It is framed, beyond, by
   two snowcapped mountains rising up from tree-
   rimmed meadows.

3. You lie, belly down, close to a rock ledge that drops
   into the foamy sea. You see the birds circling below
   and hear the roar of the waves breaking on the rock
   walls–as they have done since the dawn of time.

4. You sit by a lake that reflects the serene setting of a nearby Benedictine abbey and its turrets, lush green trees growing up the sides of nearby mountains. You hear the beautiful voices of nuns chanting the Psalter.

Prayer for Healing, Renewal, and Reconciliation: Picture Jesus laying his hand upon you and telling you that it is not by bread alone that we are satisfied (see Matthew 4:4).

Prayer of Letting Go: O God, let my concerns be washed over by the floodtide of your care and providence. At the end of this day, I am grateful for: (name one or more things).

The Our Father...

Prayer at the End of Day

Around the Celtic cross
Grow lilies of the field.
Soaring above–birds of the air.
Praise the holy Three!
Christ at the center,
The Spirit shining forth.
God a Mother–giving bread.
I belong in the very center,
Nourished, loved, and secure.
Let it be! Let it be!

Intentions: At the end of this day, I pray for: (name the people and intentions you wish to pray for).

The Magnificat...

Blessing of the Night

Blessed Be! Blessed Be!
For God "looks with favor"
On me, too!

Prayer of Affirmation: My heart is held secure at the center of the Celtic cross. I rest tonight in the arms of God.

THURSDAY

The pagan Celts believed in "thin times" and "thin places," special modes of being when times and places of our world and the spirit world came close and intersected. They practiced warm hospitality to wayfarers, whether from this world or the next.

The Christian Celts easily accommodated this to the Communion of Saints. Brigid and Patrick and the other saints are close at hand for blessings and help. Also, Christ passing from this world to the spirit world and back again felt familiar to the Celts. Holy Thursday and Ascension Thursday could be called "thin times," for Jesus offers hospitality at the Last Supper, and then makes a journey in and out and back again through the spirit world.

Morning Prayer

THE HOUR OF LAUDS

Opening Prayer: O God, come to our assistance. O God, make haste to help us. Glory to the One in Three as it was in the beginning, is now, and evermore shall be.

Hymn

Christ to shield me today
Against poison, against burning,
Against drowning, against wounding,
So that there may come to me abundance of reward.
Christ with me, Christ before me, Christ behind me,
Christ in me, Christ beneath me, Christ above me,
Christ on my right, Christ on my left,
Christ when I lie down,
Christ when I sit down,
Christ when I arise,
Christ in the heart of everyone who thinks of me,
Christ in the mouth of everyone who speaks of me,
Christ in every eye that sees me,
Christ in every ear that hears me.

I arise today
Through a mighty strength, the invocation of
    the Trinity,
Through belief in the threeness,

Through confession of the oneness,
Of the Creator of Creation.

Saint Patrick's Breastplate

Psalm

Adonai, you are my shepherd—
    I want nothing more.
You let me lie down in green meadows,
    you lead me beside restful waters:
    you refresh my soul.
You guide me to lush pastures
    for the sake of your Name.
Even if I'm surrounded by shadows of Death,
    I fear no danger,
    for you are with me.
Your rod and your staff—
    they give me courage.
You spread a table for me
    in the presence of my enemies,
and you anoint my head with oil—
    my cup overflows!
Only goodness and love will follow me
    all the days of my life,
and I will dwell in your house, Adonai,
    for days without end.

Psalm 23

Meditative Moment: Think for a moment of breakfast
and the sufficient food you will have—enough to sustain
you. Do not take it for granted, for many others rise today
with no food to satisfy or sustain them. Thanks be to God
for an abundant table.

Morning Offering: This morning, with all creation, I join
in joyful praise. I ask this blessing for the day: (add your
special intention for today).

Prayer at Rising (Option A)

Jesus, you served the best wine at Cana.
On Thursday, you sat your friends at table.
On Thursday, you washed their feet.
On Thursday, you told us to do likewise.
On Thursday, you passed through thin times
    and places.
This Thursday, I rejoice that you are with us still—
The space between us, very thin.
Wherever two or three gather,
Let us be fed by your word,
Nourished by your love.

Prayer at Rising (Option B)

Give us O God, of the morning meal,
Benefit to the body, the frame of the soul;
Give us, O God, of the seventh bread,
Enough for our need at evening close.

Give us, O God, of the honey-sweet foaming milk,
The sap and milk of the fragrant farms,
And give us, O God, along with Thy sleep,
Rest in the shade of Thy covenant Rock.

Give us this night of the corn that shall last,
Give us this night of the drink that shall hurt not;
Give us this night, anear to the heavens,
The chalice of Mary mild, the tender.

Be with us by day, be with us by night,
Be with us by light and by dark,
In our lying down and in our rising up,
In speech, in walk, in prayer.

"THE MEAL,"
Carmina Gadelica, Vol. III, p. 313, v. 1-4

Midday Prayer

Raphael, guardian of the journey and angel of God,
my guardian dear, bless my health and give me also
a safe journey to my loved ones.

Scripture Reading
Raphael answered, "I will go with him; so do not fear. We
shall leave in good health and return to you in good
health, because the way is safe."

Tobit 5:16

The Hail Mary...

Silence: Relax for a few moments and let go of the
morning. Close your eyes and take several deep breaths
until you feel your body relaxing.

Blessing of Self: I affirm and congratulate myself for...

Lunch Blessing
Bless my Thursday with a grateful heart.
Bless the tired feet of waiters and waitresses.
Bless all dishwashers and cleaners.
Bless all who wash the feet of disciples.

Bless all who share bread with the hungry poor.
Bless those who gather.
Bless the breaking of bread.
Blessed Be! Blessed Be! Blessed Be!
Christ at every table,
Christ beside me,
Christ behind me,
Christ around me,
In the breaking of the bread.

NIGHT PRAYER

THE HOUR OF COMPLINE

Opening Prayer: O God, come to our assistance. O God, make haste to help us. Glory to the One in Three as it was in the beginning, is now, and evermore shall be.

Hymn

Céad Míle Fáilte!
A hundred thousand
Welcomes to everyone!
Ever since Judas left–
Empty space at the holy table–
There is always room for more
Coming through our doors.

Sit down angel friends.
Sit down Cana couple.
Sit down Martha and Mary.
Sit down Patrick and "Bride."
Sit down guest and stranger.
Sit down poor and homeless.

Jesus comes to wash our feet.
Jesus comes to dry them well.
Jesus comes to pour our wine.
Jesus comes to break our bread.
Jesus comes to heal our wounds.
Jesus comes to lead our song.

A thin place tween living and dead.
A thin place tween love and hate.
A thin place tween friend and stranger.
A thin place tween young and old.
A thin place tween home and altar.
A thin place tween now and heaven.

A thin time! A thin place! Tween the
"Holy Banquet,
in which Christ is received,
the soul is filled with grace,
and there is given to us
a pledge of future glory!"

*(quoted material from O Sacrum Convivium,
Thomas Aquinas)*

Meditative Moment in a Celtic Land

O God, let me calm down so that I might ease into the quiet of this night. (Close your eyes. Relax your body. Be peaceful. Imagine that you are sitting in one of these scenes. Simply remain peaceful in the scene for several minutes.)

1. You look out at the highlands from a great distance. There is a patch that looks like snow—but it is a flock of sheep. There are several quilted patches of purple—heather blessing the hills.

2. You sit beside a loch, its waters offering black reflections of mountains and trees. The rippling waters are framed by green woods. A gentle rain patters on the water.

3. In heavily wooded mountains, you rest under a tree next to a stone oratory with a stone roof. A round tower points skyward. Nearby, an ancient cemetery with Celtic crosses keeps quiet watch. Some crosses are tilted with age. A soft rain falls, and a mist hovers near the still ground–a thin time, a thin place.

4. You sit beside a mountain lake at sunset, next to a fisherman's moored rowboat. You see the red of the sky reflected on the water with the black outlines of mountains against the twilight sky. Shadows hint of mysterious creatures watching you–fish, perhaps, just below the surface, or deer behind the trees.

Prayer for Healing, Renewal, and Reconciliation: Imagine Jesus washing your feet. Can you accept him doing that for you? Can you do it for others, even those who bring stress to your days (see John 13:5)?

Prayer of Letting Go: O God, let the cares of this day flow away from me like the mist rising from the still ground. At the end of this day, I am grateful for: (name one or more things).

The Our Father...

Prayer at the End of Day

Christ with me sleeping,
Christ with me waking,
Christ with me watching,

Every day and night,
Each day and night.

"GOD WITH ME LYING DOWN,"
Carmina Gadelica, Vol. I, p. 5, v. 2

Intentions: At the end of this day, I pray for: (name the people and intentions you wish to pray for).

The Magnificat...

Blessing of the Night

You have filled me, too,
With spiritual gifts and with food,
When I have been hungry!

Prayer of Affirmation: At this thin time between heaven and earth, I commend myself to good spirits who hover close.

FRIDAY

Celtic spirituality is paradoxical. In early Celtic Christian times saints fasted and sometimes stood for hours in cold water to discipline their passions. "Patrick's Purgatory" and the "white martyrdom" mirror the desert spirituality of John the Baptist.

Through the centuries, however, there was wonderful table hospitality among the Celts, a sense of celebration, night feasts with stories told and laughter shared—more in the tradition of Jesus, who loved to go to parties. Could it be that the presence of Christ was so close to their hearths and so often on their lips that they felt, "Why fast while the bridegroom is still with us?"

MORNING PRAYER

THE HOUR OF LAUDS

Perhaps the discipline of penance for our modern day
is dealing with the stress of work and carving out of
our busy lives time to practice the corporal and
spiritual works of mercy.

Opening Prayer: O God, come to our assistance. O God,
make haste to help us. Glory to the One in Three as it was
in the beginning, is now, and evermore shall be.

Hymn

I see his blood upon the rose
and in the stars the glory of his eyes.
His body gleams amid eternal snows.
His tears fall from the skies.

I see his face in every flower.
The thunder and the singing of the birds
are but his voice
and carven by his power
rocks are his written words.

All pathways by his feet are worn.
His strong heart stirs the ever-beating sea.

His crown of thorns is twined with every thorn.
His cross is every tree.

"I See His Blood upon the Rose,"
Joseph Mary Plunkett

Psalm

O God, have mercy on me!
Because of your love and your great compassion,
    wipe away my faults;
wash me clean of my guilt,
    purify me of my sin.
For I am aware of my faults,
    and have my sin constantly in mind.
I sinned against you alone,
    and did what is evil in your sight.
You are just when you pass sentence on me,
    blameless when you give judgment.

Purify me with hyssop until I am clean;
    wash me until I am purer than new-fallen snow.
Instill some joy and gladness into me,
    let the bones you have crushed rejoice again.
Turn your face from my sins,
    and wipe out all my guilt.

O God, create a clean heart in me,
    put into me a new and steadfast spirit;
do not banish me from your presence,
    do not deprive me of your holy Spirit!
Be my savior again, renew my joy,
    keep my spirit steady and willing;
and I will teach transgressors your ways,
    and sinners will return to you.

Save me from bloodshed, O God, God of my salva-
tion—
    and my tongue will acclaim your justice.
Open my lips, Adonai,
    and my mouth will declare your praise.
Sacrifice gives you no pleasure;
      were I to present a burnt offering,
      you would not have it.
My sacrifice, O God, is a broken spirit;
      you will not scorn this crushed and broken heart.

Psalm 51:1-4, 7-17

Meditative Moment: Pause to consider the meaning and mystery of pain—your own and the pain of countless millions around the world.

Morning Offering: This morning, this Cross day, I recall those who are sick, homebound, or suffering any loss. For these crossbearers, I ask God's blessing.

Prayer at Rising (Option A)

At Friday's dawning,
A moment to ponder
Today's spirituality:
Penance? discipline?
Our connecting to the Cross?

Celts knelt in cold water!
We are in hot water!
Hot tempers, frayed nerves,
Feverish consumption.
We pray, "Let go!"

At work's crossroads,
Crossbearers all around,
Hurting ones I meet today,
Also sick and suffering,
All pierced by life's wounds.

The spaces between
Cross and hospitality
Are measured very thin.
Good thief from the cross,
Banquet entered in!

Prayer at Rising (Option B)

The hand of Bride about my neck,
The hand of Mary about my breast,
The hand of Michael laving me,
The hand of Christ saving me.

Force in my mouth,
Sense be in my speech,
The taste of nectar on my lips,
Till I return hither.

> *"THE LUSTRATION," Carmina Gadelica,*
> *Vol. I, p. 59, v. 4-5 (verse 5 a variant)*

May I accept the shadow of the Cross
When it falls across my days,
For I know that someday shadows will pass away.
Brigid, lightbearer, and holy women
Who stood at the Cross,
Be with me when Fridays are dark.

The form of the Cross is upon me,
But the radiant form of the Risen Christ goes before me!
Christ in all his glory casts no shadow!
He has died. But he is risen! And he will come again!

Midday Prayer

May we never overlook the hungry in today's world.

Scripture Reading

Then Jesus was led into the desert by the Spirit, to be tempted by the Devil. After fasting for forty days and forty nights, Jesus was hungry.

...Jesus said to the Devil, "Away with you, Satan! Scripture says, 'You will worship the Most High God; God alone will you adore.'"

At that the Devil left, and angels came and attended Jesus.
Matthew 4:1-2, 10-11

The Hail Mary...

Silence: Relax for a few moments and let go of the morning. Close your eyes and take several deep breaths until you feel your body relaxing.

Blessing of Self: I affirm and congratulate myself for...

Lunch Blessing

"Blessed are those who hunger and thirst for justice:
     they will have their fill.

Blessed are those who show mercy to others:
    they will be shown mercy" (Matthew 5:6-7).

Bless those who gather.
Bless the breaking of bread.
Blessed Be! Blessed Be! Blessed Be!
Christ at every table,
Christ beside me,
Christ behind me,
Christ around me,
In the breaking of the bread.

SUNSET PRAYER

THE HOUR OF VESPERS

A common Gaelic greeting is "God is here!"

Opening Prayer: O God, come to our assistance. O God, make haste to help us. Glory to the One in Three as it was in the beginning, is now, and evermore shall be.

Hymn

> The love and affection of the angels be to you,
> The love and affection of the saints be to you,
> The love and affection of heaven be to you,
>> To guard you and to cherish you.
> May God shield you on every steep,
> May Christ aid you on every path,
> May Spirit fill you on every slope,
>> On hill and on plain.

"BLESSINGS,"
Carmina Gadelica, Vol. III, p. 207

Meditative Moment in a Celtic Land

O God, let me calm down so that I might ease into the quiet of this night. (Close your eyes. Relax your body. Be peaceful. Imagine that you are sitting quietly in one of these scenes. Simply remain peaceful in the scene for several minutes.)

1. You sit on a terrace overlooking the beautifully manicured eighteenth green of a golf course. The roughs are rough, indeed–grass high enough to wave in the breeze. It is twilight and the last foursome is putting on the final green.

2. You stand at the crossroads of a quiet countryside. With a thick green hedge as background, a signpost indicates nearby communities. Signs read: "Middleton 29"; "Tallow 12"; "Lismore 6." The bottom sign reads: "Knockmealdown Drive!" But there is no traffic, no noise, only a peaceful cross-roads.

3. You stand in front of a whitewashed, thatch-roofed pub in the green mountains. It's twilight, and wafts of blue peat smoke climb from the pub's chimney. A sign offers "Welcome."

4. You stand near a sacred well watched over by a stone carving of the mother of Saint David. She has a striking figure and looks down upon the well with a gracious smile.

Prayer for Healing, Renewal, and Reconciliation: Picture Jesus at the home of Martha, Mary, and Lazarus, with his feet up, relaxing. Welcome him (see Luke 10:38).

Prayer of Letting Go: Thank God it's Friday! Thank God it's Friday! Thank you, God, it's Friday. I praise you for this week's work, and I am grateful for: (name one or more things).

The Our Father...

Prayer at the End of Day

May the sun go down
    on anger, stress, and worry.
May the sun go down
    on problem solving and planning.
May the sun go down
    on rush and on deadlines.
May the sun go down
    on this week's work—now done.
May the sacred circle of the sun
    frame the harsh outline of the Cross.
May it signal brighter days ahead,
    new energies and emerging hopes.

Intentions: At the end of this day, I pray for: (name the people and intentions you wish to pray for).

The Magnificat...

Blessing of Twilight

Blessed Be! Blessed Be!
This sunsetting twilight time,
When once so long ago
Mary lit the Sabbath candles
In the home at Nazareth.

Prayer of Affirmation: TGIF! Thank God It's Friday!
The work week sets with the sun. I am letting go of work. I am letting go of busyness.

SATURDAY

The ancient Celts had a close affinity to the dark and the sensual. They were in touch with the dark, moist, and fertile soil. Their senses were finetuned to Earth's life force. The pagan Celts considered their holy wells to be openings into the womb of Mother Earth. Sexuality was a fruit bestowed by a generous goddess. Even the name for Ireland–Eire–derives from one of the three mother goddesses of fertility and life: Eriu.

The Christian Celts, for the greater part of two millennia, were neither puritanical nor dualistic. They were close to the Earth's cycles of fertility. They saw the Earth as good, sexuality as good, life as good–all being generous blessings. The Celts have always been "night people" as well– the night being a holy time for storytellers, song, and mirth. Celtic poets went into the holy dark to seek its blessings and hone their craft.

MORNING PRAYER

THE HOUR OF LAUDS

Opening Prayer: O God, come to our assistance. O God, make haste to help us. Glory be to the One in Three as it was in the beginning, is now, and evermore shall be.

Hymn

Come Saturday Morning–
Blessed rest, soothing sleep,
Sensuous lolling about,
Sweet sighing and yawning.

Come Saturday Morning–
Slowly emerging from the night,
Sweet scents for bathing,
Unhurried–breaking fast.

Come Saturday Morning–
Mending of the hearth,
Sweeping out all the clutter
Of a full spent week.

Come Saturday Evening–
Friends mingling and laughing,
Lovers snuggling close,
Holy night of sense delight.

Blessed be entertainment.
Blessed be fun and games.
Blessed be sounds of music.
Blessed be recreating.

Living life, savoring food,
Seeing, moving, hearing,
Making friends—or making love,
Blessed be! Blessed be!

Canticle

God of our ancestors, God of mercy,
you who have made all things by your word
and in your wisdom have established us
to care for the creatures produced by you,
to govern the world in holiness and justice,
and to render judgment in integrity of heart.

Give us Wisdom, the attendant at your throne,–
and reject us not from among your children;
for we are your servants; weak and short-lived
and lacking in comprehension of judgment and of laws.
Indeed, though some be perfect among all the peoples
    of this earth,
if Wisdom, who comes from you, be not with them,
they shall be held in no esteem.

Now with you is Wisdom, who knows your works
and was present when you made the world;
who understands what is pleasing in your eyes
and what is conformable with your commands.

Send her forth from your holy heavens—
and from your glorious throne dispatch her
that she may be with us and work with us,
that we may know what is your pleasure.

For she knows and understands all things,
and will guide us discreetly in our affairs
and safeguard us by her glory.

Wisdom 9:1-6, 9-11

Meditative Moment: Pause to look at your entire body in the mirror. Thank God for this holy temple of the Spirit. Thank God for your senses that put you in touch with the whole universe and all its glory. Blessed be your body, your senses, your sexuality, your wonderful flesh!

Morning Offering: This morning, with all creation, I join in joyful praise. I ask this blessing for the day: (add your special intention for today).

Prayer at Rising (Option A)

This morning I recall:
The holy women of Kildare.
They kept the flame alive
At Brigid's holy shrine.
It has always been so!
Women bring life and light
From the holy dark!
On the first Easter morning,
Women braved the dark and saw the light!
Holy Easter women in the garden,

And "Bride's" fire keepers of Kildare,
Bless our Saturday's coming forth.
Lead us through a blooming garden
Toward Sunday's great delights.
Help us to know the God who is in everything,
And the God who is beyond all things.
Flood our senses with goodness.
Brighten our weekend with God's long hand.

Prayer at Rising (Option B)

O God, you endowed the Celts
With keen senses and great imagination,
Seeing and sensing more than meets the eye:
Wee people—fairies, leprechauns,
Out there, all around!

Help us to have discerning eyes,
For TV images "out there"
Speeding through the air!
Heroes, villains, long-dead stars
Are out there and then—in here!

Blessed be mysteries unraveling.
Blessed be dancing and singing.
Blessed be drama and storytelling.
Blessed be athletes performing.
Blessed be worlds connecting.
Cursed be prurient pandering.
Cursed be greed manipulating.
Cursed be violence unrelenting.
Cursed be illusions lying.
Cursed be hope depleting.

O God, help us to discern the difference
Between blessings and curses,
Soul feeding and soul depleting,
Transforming and mesmerizing,
Quality and mediocrity.

Midday Prayer

Jesus relaxed on the Sabbath. Even after the cross,
on Saturday, he slept–only to come out again,
new and transformed. I pray this weekend will
be transforming and energizing.

Scripture Reading

"Why are you weeping?"

John 20:13

The Hail Mary...

Silence: Relax for a few moments before moving on to
more Saturday activity. Close your eyes and take several
deep breaths until you feel your body relaxing.

Blessing of Self: I affirm and congratulate myself at the
end of this week for...

Lunch Blessing

Blessed be the taste of food.
Blessed be the staff of life.
Blessed be the abundance of the market.
Blessed be the freedom to shop.

Bless those who gather.
Bless the breaking of bread.
Blessed Be! Blessed Be! Blessed Be!
Christ at every table,
Christ beside me,
Christ behind me,
Christ around me,
In the breaking of the bread.

NIGHT PRAYER

THE HOUR OF COMPLINE

Opening Prayer: O God, come to our assistance. O God, make haste to help us. Glory to the One in Three as it was in the beginning, is now, and evermore shall be.

Hymn

> Black shadows,
> Like spilled ink
> Upon parchment,
> Cover over
> Words, questions,
> Exclamations.

> Week's events
> All rolled up
> Into the night.
> Night chanting
> From distant ages:
> *Salve Regina!*

> Mary's cloak
> Enfold us.
> Jesus shroud
> Surround us.
> Holy Spirit bless
> The cave of dreams.

Meditative Moment in a Celtic Land

O God, let me calm down so that I might ease into the quiet of this night. (Close your eyes. Relax your body. Be peaceful. Imagine that you are sitting quietly in one of these scenes. Simply remain peaceful in the scene for several minutes.)

1. You rest at a wayside shrine—a holy well. There is the pleasant sound of a spring bubbling. Purple flowers grow along a nearby wall.

2. You hear the harp player in a great castle playing her soothing melodies.

3. You sit at the edge of an old stone bridge. The salmon, their silver backs visible, idle just below the water's surface.

4. You watch the pageantry of a great Scottish festival. You hear the pipes playing and see kilts swirling as the Highlanders march by.

Prayer for Healing, Renewal, and Reconciliation: Picture Jesus' empty tomb, quiet in the shadows of dawn's light. See the linen wrappings lying on the ground, touch the empty shroud, now glorious for being so close to resurrection (see John 20:6).

Prayer of Letting Go: O God, let the busyness of this day and this past week subside as I prepare to enter the joy that Sunday is meant to bring. At the end of this day, I am grateful for: (name one or more things).

The Our Father...

Prayer at the End of Day

Creative Spirit,
Take this week's jumble–
The many hours of work
And this weekend's fun–
Into the deep, dark, dream pool
Of the Salmon of Knowledge.
From my night dreaming
May fresh creative ideas
Make the "salmon's leap"
Out of the depths
Into daily life.

Intentions: At the end of this day, I pray for: (name the people and intentions you wish to pray for).

The Magnificat...

Blessing of the Night

Praise God!
For God has shown
Mercy to me, too!

Prayer of Affirmation: I enter the holy dark, the sacred land of dreams. I dream with the Spirit.

ALTERNATE PSALMS FOR MORNING PRAYER

THE HOUR OF LAUDS

Sunday: 8; 63:1-9; 93; 118; 148; 149; or 150

Monday: 19; 29; 42; 84; 90; 96; or 135

Tuesday: 24; 29; 43; 65; 67; 85; 101; or 144:1-10

Wednesday: 16; 36; 77; 86; 97; 98; 108; or 146

Thursday: 1; 48; 80; 81; 99; 143:1-11; or 147:1-11

Friday: 13; 23; 100; or 147:12-20

Saturday: 1; 8; 92; 117; or 119:145-152

ALTERNATE CANTICLES
FOR MORNING PRAYER
THE HOUR OF LAUDS

Sunday: Daniel 3:52-57; Luke 1:67-79; or Philippians 2:6-11

Monday: I Chronicles 9:10-13; Isaiah 2:2-5; Isaiah 42:10-16; or Sirach 36:1-5, 10-13

Tuesday: Isaiah 38:10-14, 17-20; Isaiah 26:1-12; Daniel 3:26-29, 34-41; or Tobit 13:1-8

Wednesday: I Samuel 2:1-10; Isaiah 33:13-16; or Isaiah 61:1-3

Thursday: Isaiah 12:1-6; Isaiah 40:1-17; Isaiah 66:10-14; or Jeremiah 31:10-14

Friday: Isaiah 45:15-25; Jeremiah 14:17-21; Habakkuk 3:2-4, 15-19; or Tobit 13:8-11, 13-15

Saturday: Ruth 1:15-18; Song of Songs 1:1-4; Song of Songs 2:1-7; or Song of Songs 2:8-17

Alternate Readings for Night Prayer

THE HOUR OF COMPLINE

The meditative Scriptures at Compline (Prayer for Healing, Renewal, and Reconciliation) for six days of the week
are devoted to comforting messages. Thursday's Compline
Scriptures focus on our need to be challenged and to
acknowledge the dark side of life and the shadow of the
cross. The following Scripture passages are divided into
"Comforting" and "Challenging" selections.

THE GOSPEL OF MATTHEW

Comforting Passages: 5:1-10 (the Beatitudes); 6:26-34
(the lilies of the field); 7-12 (ask and you shall receive); 8:1-
4 (the leper is healed); 8:5-13 (the centurion's attendant is
healed); 8:14:17 (Peter's mother-in-law is healed); 9:1-8 (a
paralytic is healed); 9:10-13 (Jesus eats with sinners); 9:20-
22 (the woman with a hemorrhage is healed); 9:35-38
(Jesus is moved with compassion); 10:29-30 (we are worth
more than sparrows); 10:40-42 (the rewards of hospitality);
11:4-6 (good news for the poor); 11:29-30 (Jesus' yoke is
easy); 12:15-21 (the bruised reed); 13:36-52 (the parables of
the seeds, the treasure, the pearls, the net); 14:13-21 (Jesus
has pity for the crowds); 15:29-31 (Jesus heals the multitude); 18:10-14 (care for children and the lost sheep);

20:29-34 (Jesus gives sight to the blind); 26:26-30 (the Last Supper); 28:1-10 (Mary of Magdala on Easter morning)

Challenging Passages: 14:25-33 (Peter is terrified on the water); 15:1-9 (Jesus challenges hypocrites); 15:10-20 (Jesus accuses the leaders of being blind); 16:22-26 (Jesus challenges us to take up our cross); 18:1-8 (Jesus challenges us to be converted like children); 18:21-35 (forgiveness); 19:23-3 (the challenges and difficulties of having riches); 20:25-28 (leaders must serve); 21:12-13 (Jesus throws money-changers out of the Temple); 21:18-22 (cursing the fig tree); 21:28-32 (tax collectors and prostitutes entering the kingdom of heaven); 22:34-46 (the Great Commandment); 23:27-39 (hypocrisy); 24:43-44 (be awake); 25:31-46 (what we do to the least—the last judgment); 26:36-46 (Jesus is grieved to the point of death); 27:45-53 (the crucifixion)

THE GOSPEL OF MARK

Comforting Passages: 1:14-15 (proclaiming the Good News); 2:1-12 (paralytic is healed); 2:15-17 (Jesus has come to call sinners); 3:1-5 (Jesus heals a person's withered hand); 5:25-34 (the woman with a hemorrhage is healed); 5:21-24 and 35-43 (Jesus heals the daughter of Jairus); 6:30-32 (the invitation to rest awhile); 6:33-34 (the sheep without a shepherd); 6:47-50 ("Do not be afraid"); 6:53-56 (Jesus touches and heals); 7:32-35 (Jesus heals those who cannot hear or speak); 8:1-9 (the multiplication of loaves and fishes); 8:22-26 (a person who is blind is healed); 9:2-8 (the Transfiguration); 10:13-16 (we must welcome the kingdom as a little child); 10:46-52 (Bartimaeus is healed); 11:22-24 (trust); 11:25 (forgiveness); 12:28-34 (the Great Commandment); 14:3-9 (Mary anoints Jesus); 14:22-26 (the Last Supper); 16:1-8 (the holy women at the Easter tomb)

Challenging Passages: 4:21-22 (don't hide light under a bushel basket); 7:6-8 (lip service); 7:14-15 (evils of the heart); 8:34-38 (take up your cross); 9:43-47 (scandal); 9:50 (if salt loses its flavor); 10:5-8 (do not divide what God has joined); 10:21-27 (hard for the rich to be saved); 10:42-45 (great ones must serve the rest); 11:15-17 (Jesus drives out money-changers); 13:32-37 (be alert); 14:37-38 (the disciples fall asleep); 15:6-15 (death sentence); 15:21 (Simon of Cyrene); 15:33 (the crucifixion)

THE GOSPEL OF LUKE

Comforting Passages: 1:67-80 (benedictus of Zechariah); 2:6-20 (the nativity); 2:29-32 (Simeon's proclamation); 2:36-38 (Anna's proclamation); 4:14-19 (mission statement of Jesus); 4:33-37 (person possessed by demon is exorcized); 4:40-41 (laying on of hands, healing); 5:4-11 (large catch of fish); 5:18-20 (person who is paralyzed is lowered from roof and healed); 5:27-32 (party for tax collectors and sinners); 6:36-37 (be compassionate); 7:11-15 (raising to life of a woman's only son); 7:21-23 (report to John of healings); 7:36-50 (woman's sins forgiven); 8:4-8 (parable of seeds); 10:29-37 (parable of Good Samaritan); 10:38-41 (Martha and Mary); 11:1-4 (the Our Father); 11:5-13 (persist in prayer); 12:22-28 (lilies of field); 12:29-33 (treasure); 13:18-21 (kingdom of God like mustard seed or leaven in dough); 13:34 (Jesus like a mother); 15:3-7 (parable of lost sheep); 15:8 (parable of lost silver pieces); 15:11-31 (Prodigal Son); 17:11-19 (gratitude of leper); 18:1-5 (parable of persistent woman); 18:9-14 (Pharisee and Publican); 18:15-17 (Jesus blesses infants); 19:1-9 (Jesus eats with Zacchaeus); 22:1-20 (the Last Supper); 23:39-43 (the good thief); 24:1-8 (the empty tomb); 24:9-12 (women as the first witnesses to the resurrection); 24:13-35 (disciples on the road to Emmaus); 24:36-47 (the Risen Jesus eats with disciples); 24:50-53 (the joy of the resurrection)

Challenging Passages: 3:3-6 (John the Baptist's call to repentance); 4:23-30 (the homecoming); 6:20-26 (the Beatitudes); 6:27-35 (love your enemies); 6:36-38 (be compassionate); 6:41:42 (the beam in the eye); 6:43-49 (practice what you preach); 9:23-25 (if you gain the world and lose your soul); 9:51-56 (Jesus rebukes violence); 9:57-62 (put your hand to the plow); 11:23-26 (with or against Jesus); 11:33-35 (let your light shine); 11:37-46 (Jesus condemns hypocrisy); 12:1-3 (nothing will be hidden); 12:16-21 (parable about the folly of riches and the sureness of death); 12:49-51 (Jesus has come to light a fire); 12:54-59 (settling grievances); 13:1-5 (change your ways); 14:12-14 (take care of the poor); 14:33-35 (possessions); 16:1-12 (parable of the shrewd steward); 16:13-14 (cannot worship both God and money); 16:19-31 (parable of rich person and Lazarus); 17:1-3 (forgiveness); 18:24 (how hard for the rich to enter the kingdom of God); 20:45-47 (beware of pretentious clergy); 21:29-31 (parable of the fig tree)

THE GOSPEL OF JOHN

Comforting Passages: 1:4-5 (Jesus the Light); 1:14-18 (sharers of Christ's glory); 1:32-34 (John's testimony); 1:35-45 (finding the Messiah); 2:1-11 (wedding at Cana); 3:1-8 (born again); 3:16-17 (God's love for the world); 4:1-10, 11-18, 19-24, 25-30 (Jesus at the well with the Samaritan woman); 4:39-42 (the witness of the Samaritan woman); 5:16-18 (Abba-Papa); 5:24-25 (eternal life); 6:35-40 (bread of life); 6:66-68 (to whom can they go?); 7:37-39 (rivers of living water); 8:2-12 (woman caught in adultery); 9:1-6 (healing of the man who is blind); 10:1-5 (the sheep and the shepherd); 10:6-18 (Jesus, the Good Shepherd); 11:1-16 (the death of Lazarus); 11:17-45 (the raising of Lazarus); 12:1-3 (woman's hospitality); 12:46-47 (Jesus has not come to condemn the world); 13:1-15 (Jesus washes the feet of the disciples); 13:33-35 (a new commandment: love one another); 14:1-4 (don't be troubled); 14:5-7 (Jesus is the Way); 14:16-21 (the Spirit will not leave disciples as orphans); 14:27-31 (do not be distressed); 15:1-5 (vine and branches); 15:7 (ask); 15:8-11 (live in love and joy); 15:12-14 (no greater love); 15:15-16 (Jesus calls us friends); 15:17-19 (love one another); 15:20-25 (persecution); 15: 26-27 (the Spirit of truth); 16:7-13 (the Paraclete will come); 16:20-22 (grief will turn to joy); 16:29-33 (Jesus overcomes the world); 17:1-10 (prayer for disciples); 17:11-13 (prayer for disciples); 17:14-26 (prayer for disciples); 19:25-27 (Mary at the cross); 20:1-10(Peter and John at the tomb); 20:11-18 (Mary of Magdala and the Risen Jesus); 20:19-22 (the Risen Jesus and forgiveness of sins); 20:24-30 (doubting Thomas); 21:1-13 (Risen Jesus at the lake); 21:15-19 (feeding the sheep)

Challenging Passages: 2:13-17 (cleansing of the Temple); 16:29-33 (disciples will suffer); 19:1-6 (Jesus is condemned); 19:28-30 (Jesus expires); 19:31-37 (Jesus is pierced)

MEDITATIVE MOMENT
IN A CELTIC LAND

Sunday

1. Stream running through Galway City
2. Powerscourt, Wicklow Mountains
3. Muckross House, Killarney, Ireland
4. Loch Shiel, Scotland

Monday

1. Bundoran in Donegal, the beach fronting the resort city
2. The statue of Saint Brendan that looks out on Bantry Bay, County Cork
3. The Kerry Coast near Dingle
4. Dingle in Kerry

Tuesday

1. Turf fire, found anywhere
2. Tara, County Meath, Ireland
3. Anywhere
4. Island of Iona between Scotland and Ireland

Wednesday

1. A Galway field
2. Kilchum Castle in Scotland
3. The view from Dun Aenghus, Inishmore, Aran Islands
4. Kylemore Abbey in Galway

Thursday

1. Scotland on the road to Edinburgh
2. Loch Lomand in Scotland
3. Saint Kevin's Oratory, Glendalough, Wicklow Mountains
4. An upper lake, Killarney in Ireland

Friday

1. Ballybunnion Golf Course, County Kerry
2. Crossroads, County Waterford
3. Pub on the road to Dublin, in the Wicklow Mountains
4. A statue of the mother of Saint David above a sacred well in Dirinon, Britanny, France

Saturday

1. Saint Non's Well, near Saint David's, Dyfed in Wales
2. Bunratty Castle in County Clare
3. River running through the city of Sligo, Ireland
4. The heights of Edinburgh, summer festival

PART II

CELTIC BLESSINGS, PRAYERS, AND RITUALS

BLESSINGS

Jesus walked a "blessing path," his greatest sermon:
the Beatitudes. Blessed be! Blessed be! Blessed be!

Blessing of a Baby

Blessed babe! Blessed babe!
Voice of Elizabeth, greet thee.
Eyes of Brigid, watch thee.
Heart of Anne, prize thee.
Breast of Mary, warm thee.

Blessed babe! Blessed babe!
Oil of Baptism, glisten thee.
Candle of Baptism, lead thee.
Robe of Baptism, garb thee.
Water of Baptism, wash thee.

Blessed babe! Blessed babe!
Holy Parent, hold thee.
Holy Spirit, breathe thee.
Holy Son, save thee.
Holy Mary, keep thee.

Blessing of a Child

Bless this child
Around your bed.
Bless this child

Encircled by faith,
Encircled by love,
Encircled by kin.

Bless this child
Encircled by Mary,
Encircled by Anne,
Encircled by "Bride."

Bless this child
Around your bed.

Blessing of Children

Bless the children—
The bloom of health,
The bloom of growth,
The bloom of cheer,
The bloom of innocence
Shine forth from thee.

Bless the children—
The grace of the deer,
The grace of the wren,
The grace of the swan,
The grace of the lamb
Move thy limbs.

Bless the children—
The sword of Michael,
The armor of Raphael,
The armor of angel hosts,
The armor of guardians
Shield thee, asleep or awake.

Blessing of Grandchildren

We are born again in our children's eyes,
In fleeting expressions—glimpses of ourselves.
Blessed be ancestry down the ages.
The many are one.
Each one is many.

We are born again in our grandchildren's eyes,
In certain gestures—glimpses of ourselves.
Blessed be ancestry down the ages.
The many are one.
Each one is many.

And yet they are apart—on their own life courses.
Bless their growing. Bless their sowing.
May their futures be better than our pasts.
The many are one.
We ourselves are many.

Blessing for a Friend

Should auld acquaintance be forgot,
    And never brought to min'?
Should auld acquaintance be forgot,
    And days o' lang syne?

"Auld Lang Syne," Robert Burns

Blessed be o' lang syne!
Blessed be o' lang syne!
Blessing upon you, my friend,
Yesterday, today, tomorrow.
Like a mellow peat fire,

Your friendship casts a glow
Into the darkest corners of my life.

Blessed be fire-tried trust.
Blessed be embers of loyalty,
Never to be snuffed out
By smothering separation,
Nor even by the winds of time.

Blessed be o' lang syne!
Blessed be o' lang syne!

Blessing for a Journey

May the road rise to meet you.
May the wind be always at your back.
May the sun shine warm upon your face.
And the rain fall soft upon your fields.
And until we meet again,
May you be held in the palm of God's hand.

Old Irish verse

Blessing for Meals

When thou takest thy food, think of Him
    who gives it, namely,
God, and whilst thinking of His Name,
    with the word put the
first morsel in thy mouth, thank God for it,
    and entreat His
grace and blessing upon it, that it may be
    for the health of
thy body and mind; then thy drink

in the same manner.
And upon any other thing or quantity,
   which thy canst not
take with the Name of God in thy mind,
   entreat His grace
and blessing, lest it should prove an injury
   and a curse to thee.

"The Mode of Taking Food and Drink,"
The Sacred World of the Celts

Blessing of a House

May God give blessing
   To the house that is here;

May Jesus give blessing
   To the house that is here;

May Spirit give blessing
   To the house that is here;

May Three give blessing
   To the house that is here.

"BLESSING OF THE HOUSE,"
Carmina Gadelica, Vol. III, p. 361, v. 1-4

Prayers to Celtic Saints

G. K. Chesterton wrote that the Celtic saints
of the Dark Ages were "like a multitude of
moving candles that lit up the world."

Prayer to the Vibrant Women of Celtic Lore

At eighty-three by the side of the sea,
She served us tea at Dun Laoghaire.
To an old tin shack,
Her friends would come back,
From one generation to three.
Her face was wrinkled and folded
Like an ancient well-used map,
But her eyes were a light,
And her smile was so bright
For all who passed by at Dun Laoghaire.

So this day, a toast and prayers
To the vibrant women of Celtic lore.

Ancient tea brewer of Dun Laoghaire,
Give me vigor for life's daily jousts.

Countess Constance, holstered rebel,
Give me courage to make my stand.

Grace O'Malley, swashbuckler,
Guide my ship through stormy seas.

Brigid of Kildare, "Bride" of the Gaels,
May your shepherd's staff lead o'er high hills.

Maeve, mythic queen of ardor,
May her memory energize us for every challenge.

Hilda of Whitby, abbess of women and men,
Join the sexes together—our world to mend.

Ita of Limerick, foster mother of Brendan,
Help us to seek the Promised Land.

Round and Round—Saints Surround Us

I walk with the saints
...Round and round.
With Patrick
...On the reek's high brow.
With Brigid
...In Kildare's town.
With Kevin
...In verdant Glendalough.
Here today
...In my own town,
Saints surround me
...Round and round!

Prayer to Saint Colm Cille

Colm Cille of Iona,
"Dove of the Church,"
And the tender healer
Of the lost and weary crane,
Your great white horse

Wept tears at your passing.
Bless the animals.
Bless the birds.
Bless the sea creatures.

Bless the barking.
Bless the meowing.
Bless the growling.
Bless the leaping.
Bless the swimming.

Bless my friendly pet,
Since all creation
Rightly gives God praise!

Prayer to Saint Patrick

Saint Patrick's Day no more we'll keep.
His color can't be seen,
for there's a bloody law against
the wearin' of the green.

"Wearing of the Green," Traditional Irish air

Once trodden down,
The green now free to grow,
On hills, in valleys, and glens.

From a hilltop in Cavan,
The hills are a rolling quilt,
A patchwork of every shade of green.

In the farthest north,
Green velvet hills roll to the sea,
And drop down into Giants' Causeway.

In the green glens of Antrim,
Sparkling streams flow,
Their silver threads the green.

Like some dyer using batik,
God has dipped this land
In glorious emerald hues.

It was so with Patrick,
His heart and soul
Bathed in Erin's green.

Patrick, enslaved and set free,
Bless green growing shoots
Rooted very deep in my dark.

Patrick, shamrock in hand,
Give a threefold blessing,
For heart, hearth, and work.

Patrick, resting at Down,
Spread your peace like a mantle
O'er every troubled land.

Prayer to Saint Columbanus and Other "Green Saints"

Saint Columbanus, help our minds to wander
Through nature's beauty all around and beyond.
Saint Columbanus, companion and lover of animals
    and birds,
Bless the creatures that brighten our days.
Saint Columbanus, intrepid traveler,
Guide us on our journeys near and far.
Saint Columbanus, lover of the forest,

Help us to be healed by green trees and plants.
Saint Hildegard of Bingen,
Bless our rain forests and the green circle of life.
Saint Clare, lover of the quiet countryside,
Deliver us from rush, rage, and stress.
Saint Francis, deepen our kinship with all creation.
Let us be instruments of peace on God's green earth.
All you holy saints who slaked your thirsts at
    Celtic wells,
Hear our prayer.

Prayers for Special Intentions

There is a Gaelic saying expressing nostalgic yearnings:
God be with the days.

God Be with the Days

In my heart and mind,
I make a holy circle,
Pilgrimage around
The lands of saints and scholars,
And I seek answers to these petitions.

I journey to Edinburgh's royal hill.
Saint Margaret, Queen of the Scots,
I ask three times for this petition.
I ask three times for this petition.
I ask three times for this petition.

I journey to Dublin's Georgian doors.
Mother McAuley of Mercy,
I ask three times for this petition.
I ask three times for this petition.
I ask three times for this petition.

I journey to outstretched arms at Bantry Bay.
Saint Brendan, seeker and searcher,

I ask three times for this petition.
I ask three times for this petition.
I ask three times for this petition.

I journey to Croagh Patrick's peak,
To famine's ship beneath his feet.
I ask three times for this petition.
I ask three times for this petition.
I ask three times for this petition.

I journey to Saint Brigid's shrine,
And circle round your staff and spring.
I ask three times for this petition.
I ask three times for this petition.
I ask three times for this petition.

I journey round to Knock's town square,
Where candles flicker at Mary's feet.
I ask three times for this petition.
I ask three times for this petition.
I ask three times for this petition.

I journey round Scripture and verse.
I journey round Christ in our midst.
Holy Father, hear your saints.
Holy Spirit, bring a response.
Holy Son, let it be; let it be.

Prayer of the Divorced

The woman said to Jesus,
"Give me this water" (John 4:15).

The holy wells of Ireland and Wales!
The holy wells of Scotland!

The holy well of Samaria!
All openings to the womb of Mother Earth!

Jesus, I sometimes feel alone at life's well.
I feel alone drawing the waters of sustenance.
I feel alone drawing the waters of refreshment.
Am I alone drawing water that nourishes my soul?

"No my child, you are not alone.
I sat with the woman at the Samaritan well,
And she was many times divorced.
I had time for her and then sent her with good news.

Drink from Brigid's Well with blest women of all ages.
Drink from Patrick's Well with blest men of all ages.
Drink from the Samaritan Well—with me!
Then take life-giving water to others who are alone."

Prayer of Single Parents

Saint Michael the Archangel,
Protector of the monks of Skellig Michael,
Hear the prayers of single moms and dads.
We, too, live in beehive dwellings.
We are the "busy bees" of family life.

Like a solitary lighthouse,
Each single parent must point the way.
Saint Michael, leader of the heavenly host,
Light the path for us; show us the way
Through darkest night and brightest day.

Give us energy for double duty.
Protect our hearth. Protect our health.

Protect our children. Protect our work.
May we dwell on rock, not shifting sands.
Bless this day and bless our double work.

Prayer for Caretakers

Catherine McAuley, Spirit-gifted,
Your arms open wide for mercy,
Strengthen our weary arms.
Pray for us when spirits sag.

Saint Brigid, patroness of holy wells,
Open to caretakers wells of fresh water.
Saint Brigid, spirited fire keeper,
Tend the Spirit's flame in our hearts.

Holy Spirit, Consoler and Sustainer,
Buoy up all caretakers on the rough seas of suffering.
Great enabling Spirit, take care of caretakers.

Give us energy to stand by as long as we can,
And then to let go of our loved ones to others' care
When we are depleted and cannot do our best.

Holy Spirit, you care for us!
Holy Parent, you shelter us!
Holy Son, you shepherd us!

PRAYERS FOR THE SHADOW TIMES: SICKNESS

Blessed are the holy hands of healers;
their touch leaves the fingerprints of the Christ.

For the Healing of an Addiction, One Day at a Time

This day I have within me the resolve of Matt Talbot.
This day I have within me the discipline of Brigid.
This day I have within me the triune faith of Patrick.
This day I have within me the courage of Brendan.

This day a pilgrimage,
One step at a time.
Let me walk with Matt Talbot
And the pioneers of sobriety.

This day a pilgrimage,
One step at a time.
Let me walk with Brigid,
Her staff a guide and discipline.

This day a pilgrimage,
One step at a time.

Let me walk with Patrick,
His Breastplate, my daily shield.

This day a pilgrimage,
One step at a time.
Let me sail with Brendan,
Safe, sober, and clean at day's end.

Sevenfold Blessings for Those Who Are Sick

First—from the east—a rising good fortune.
Second—from the west—a waning of worry.
Third—from the north—a cooling of fever.
Fourth—from the south—a soothing breeze.
Fifth—from the Father—a house secure.
Sixth—from the Spirit—a full breathing.
Seventh—from the Son—a healing touch.

Jesus, keeper of all our days,
Bring your healing touch.
Cast out illness, restore health.
Saint Brigid and Saint Patrick, be near;
Bless doctors, nurses, and caretakers.
From east, west, north, south, send new life—
O God, send your Shalom on the seventh day.

Healing Blessings from Holy Wells

From the Lake of Innisfree—peace and healing!
From Brigid's holy well—peace and healing!
From Lourdes holy spring—peace and healing!
From Siloam's holy pool—peace and healing!

From the holy well of our faith and trust,
New hope for better days.
From the holy well of patience,
Endurance till better days come.

Jesus, keeper of the holy wells,
Let us draw up energy.
Jesus, your well of love is deep.
Let us draw up healing.

Horses of Healing

Good health gallops full speed,
Like a pony colt of Connemara.
Heavy burdens and illness
Slow even the mighty Clydesdale.
Sickness is the bridle of halting.
Jesus, rider of donkeys
And tender of wounded sheep,
Lead us to green pastures of healing.

PRAYERS FOR THE THIN TIMES: DEATH AND MOURNING

Derry Air

O Danny Boy, if you should come and I am dead,
as dead I well may be,
you'll come and find the place where I am lying,
and kneel and say an "Ave" there for me.
And I shall hear, though soft you tread above me.

Adapted from "Derry Air," Fred E. Weatherly

Irish Wake Prayer: Our Lady of the Wake

Wake time, sorrow-sharing time.
Wake time, storytelling time.
Wake time, vigil-keeping time.
Wake time, embracing time.

Lady of the Wake, our life;
Lady of the Wake, our sweetness;
Lady of the Wake, our hope in loss;
Lady of the Wake, our refuge in tears.

Wake time, a thin time.
Wake time, in a thin place.
Wake time, tears and laughter very close.
Wake time, here and hereafter closer still.

Lady of the Wake, you waked Mama Anne.
Lady of the Wake, you waked Papa Joachim.
Lady of the Wake, you waked beloved Joseph.
Lady of the Wake, you waked your own dear Son.

Lady of Sorrows, hear the keening.
Lady of Sorrows, bless our stories.
Lady of Sorrows, smile at our laughter.
Lady of Sorrows, keep watch with us.

Queen of Heaven reach through thin time.
Queen of Heaven reach beyond death's time.
Queen of Heaven you were there at death's parting.
Queen of Heaven now give to our loved one
    glory' greeting.

Prayer for the Dying

Thou goest home this night to thy home of winter,
To thy home of autumn, of spring, and of summer;
Thou goest home this night to thy perpetual home,
To thine eternal bed, to thine eternal slumber.

> Sleep thou, sleep, and away with thy sorrow,
> Sleep thou, sleep, and away with thy sorrow,
> Sleep thou, sleep, and away with thy sorrow;
> Sleep, thou beloved, in the Rock of the fold.

Sleep this night in the breast of thy Mother,
Sleep, thou beloved, while she herself soothes thee;
Sleep thou this night on the Virgin's arm,
Sleep, thou beloved, while she herself kisses thee.

122

The great sleep of Jesus, the surpassing sleep of Jesus,
The sleep of Jesus' wound, the sleep of Jesus' grief,
The young sleep of Jesus, the restoring sleep of Jesus,
The sleep of the kiss of Jesus of peace and of glory.

"THE DEATH DIRGE,"
Carmina Gadelica, Vol. III, p. 353, v. 1-4

The Harvest Is with Christ

The seed is with Christ
And the harvest is with Christ.
May we be gathered into God's granary.

The sea is with Christ
And the fish are with Christ.
May we be swept into God's nets.

From growth to maturity,
And from maturity to death,
May you, O Christ,
Close your arms tightly around us!

From death to finish—oh, it is not finish,
But a new growth.
May we be found dwelling
In the paradise of the graced!

Traditional Gaelic prayer

PRAYERS FOR THE MOONTIMES: LOVE AND ROMANCE

Anam Cara

> For my beloved:
> Holy Trinity
> Sacred Threesome
> One and Two
> Love makes Three!
>
> For my beloved:
> Deep Spirit whispering
> Soothe thee
> Warm thee
> Guard thee.
>
> For my beloved:
> Deep dark imaging
> Intuit thee
> Dream thee
> Thou—Me.
>
> For my beloved:
> Depth of soul stirring
> Touch thee
> Link thee

Pray thee.
For my beloved:
Anam cara
Woo thee
Wed thee
Bed thee.

For my beloved:
Holy Trinity
Sacred Threesome
One and Two
Love makes Three.

Divine Allurement–Blessed Passions

Divine allurement fills the universe.
The moon calls out to the tides.
Streams, rivers, oceans,
Hug the earth and run their course.
Mountains, hills, and crests–
Paps of the Earth Mother's breasts.
     Blessed be love's sweet wine!

Love springs from ancient earth
When harvest comes from the vine.
Fertile seedbed of yearning,
Grapes of love–the sweetest wine!
     Blessed be my beloved!

My beloved–a vintage choice,
Our passions–vines intertwined–
Must be tended daily
While life's juices run.
Blessed be passion!

Bless our passions,
You saints of heaven,
Around three times
Our lovers' bed.

Prayer to the Divine Marriage Broker

Marriage Broker, make me a match!
Fire of triune love,
Let me move from one to three:
I–You–and she/he.

Marriage Broker, make me a match!
For I believe deep in my heart
It were better for me to be three:
I–You–and she/he.

Marriage Broker, make me a match!
Surely you allured Joseph to Mary!
It was better for them to be two,
And Jesus made three.

Marriage Broker, make me a match!
If I ask for a mate,
Will I be given a stone?
My prayer is not to be alone.

CYCLES OF THE
EARTH AND CHURCH:
PRAYERS AND RITUALS

The four walls of the seasons provide the
frames for our life's pictures.

Prayer for Advent

In the Word was life,
 and that life was humanity's light—
a Light that shines in the darkness,
 a Light that the darkness has never overtaken.

John 1:4-5

O God, in ancient Decembers,
In the narrow corridor at Newgrange,
Ancestors huddled very low,
Yearning for the solstice sun.
We, too, wait—but for the Son.
We wait expectantly in the pregnant, holy dark.
We wait in joyful hope for the advent of our Savior.

Let the Christ light penetrate into the inner corridors
 of our hearts.

Where there is darkness, let there be light.
Where there is coldness, let there be warmth.
Where there is doubt, let there be hope.
Where there is guilt, let there be forgiveness.
Maranatha! Come, Lord Jesus!

Prayer for Lent

Remember that you are dust,
and unto dust you shall return.

Ash Wednesday Blessing

"The Old Sod!"
The precious land!
The sacred earth!

Ash Wednesday's smudge
Remember we are earth
And we shall return.

Jesus is of earth
Every bone and sinew
The Word enfleshed.

His beginning sacred
A holy earth birthing
A heavenly ending.

Our Lenten journey
Wednesday's blest earth
To Easter's blest water!

And we are more than
"Dust in the wind."
We are bound for glory!

O God, bless my Lenten journey.
Let me walk the blessing path of Jesus.
Blessed be the path of giving.
Blessed be the path of discipling.
Blessed be the garden of grieving.
Blessed be the mountain of the cross.
Blessed be these forty days.

May I be more loving, more generous,
More forgiving, more grateful,
As I trod the desert path
Leading to Easter's water–
A fountain springing up
Toward eternal life!

A Ritual for the Feast of Saint Brigit

(February 1. You will need reeds, toothpicks, or straws–
long ones and short ones–and a candle. This celebration
corresponds to Candlemas and the ancient Celtic Imbolc
festival.)

LEADER: We gather at the edge of spring, the last gasps
of winter. Our Lenten journey shall be from fertile and
holy dirt, smudged on our foreheads on Ash Wednesday,
to the lively and leaping waters of Easter rebirth.

We light this candle, remembering that, for almost a
millennium, a perpetual flame was tended at Brigit's shrine
in Kildare, and that the hearth fire was considered to be a

spiritual gift from Brigit. We light this candle as a reminder of Mary's feast and the goodness bestowed by God upon all women.

As we prepare to make Saint Brigit's cross with reeds, (toothpicks or straws) we are encouraged by the words of Jesus: "You will not break the bruised reed or snuff out the smoldering wick" (Matthew 12:20).

Springtime—Lent—is always a new beginning. Let us hold our reed in hand and consider what bruised reed we bring today to Brigit's cross. (Allow a few minutes of silent reflection. If the assembly would like to share their reflections, invite each person to begin with "The bruised reed I bring today is....")

We walk with Brigit. We ask her blessing as we remake Saint Brigit's cross. Let us pray.

ALL:

    Cross, cross, Brigit and her cross,
    Mary and her Son,
    Brigit and her cloak,
    Good as we are today,
    May we be seven times better
    A year from now.

Traditional Celtic prayer

(Each member places a reed around the lit candle. Place all short reeds at 12:00, 3:00, and 9:00 positions. Place the longer reeds at 6:00. The pattern will be that of a cross with a lit candle at the cross beams.)

LEADER: Let us pray the Blessing of Brigit.

ALL:

I shall not be slain,
    I shall not be sworded,
I shall not be put in cell,
    I shall not be hewn,
I shall not be riven,
    I shall not be anguished,
I shall not be wounded,
    I shall not be ravaged,
I shall not be blinded,
    I shall not be made naked,
I shall not be left bare,

Nor will Christ
    Leave me forgotten.

        Nor fire shall burn me,
        Nor sun shall burn me,
        Nor moon shall blanch me.

        Nor water shall drown me,
        Nor flood shall drown me,
        Nor brine shall drown me.

        Nor seed of fairy host shall lift me,
        Nor seed of airy host shall lift me,
        Nor earthly being destroy me.

I am under the shielding
    Of good Brigit each day;

I am under the shielding
>Of good Brigit each night.
I am under the keeping
>Of the Nurse of Mary,
Each early and late,
>Every dark, every light.

Brigit is my comrade-woman,
>Brigit is my maker of song,
Brigit is my helping-woman,
>My choicest of women, my woman of guidance.

"BLESSING OF BRIGIT,"
Carmina Gadelica, Vol. III, p. 161

A Ritual for May Day

(May 1. You will need a statue of Mary and flowers. Begin this ritual by singing an appropriate hymn to Mary, such as "O Mary We Crown Thee with Blossoms Today.")

LEADER: Let us bless others with new energy and life.

(One by one, those assembled offer the blessing: "Those I wish to bless with new energy and life are....")

LEADER: Let us pray the "Beltane Blessing."

MARRIED COUPLES:

Bless, O Threefold true and bountiful,
Myself, my spouse, and my children,
My tender children and their beloved mother at
>their head.

On the fragrant plain, on the gay mountain sheiling,
On the fragrant plain, on the gay mountain sheiling.

UNMARRIED INDIVIDUALS:

Everything within my dwelling or in my possession,
All kine and crops, all flocks and corn,
From Hallow Eve to Beltane Eve,
With goodly progress and gentle blessing.
From sea to sea, and every river mouth,
From wave to wave, and base of waterfall.

ALL:

Be the Three Persons taking possession of all to
    me belonging.
Be the sure Trinity protecting me in truth;
Oh! satisfy my soul in the words of Paul,
And shield my loved ones beneath the wing of
    Thy glory,
Shield my loved ones beneath the wing of Thy glory.

Bless everything and every one,
Of this little household by my side;
Place the cross of Christ on us with the power of love,
Till we see the land of joy,
Till we see the land of joy.

> *"BELTANE BLESSING,"*
> *Carmina Gadelica, Vol. I, p. 183, v. 1-4*

(Form a circle and move in a clockwise direction, walking
or skipping–as to a Celtic lilt–while singing this famous
American Shaker Song.)

ALL SING:

> 'Tis a gift to be simple.
> 'Tis a gift to be free.
> 'Tis a gift to come down
> Where we ought to be.
> And when we find ourselves
> In the valley of delight,
> Turning, turning
> Come around right!

(Keeping hands joined and raising them, move toward the center of the circle. At the center, raise joined hands high and sing:)

> When true simplicity is gained...

(Let go of hands, keep arms raised, back up a step or two, bow toward the center, and sing:)

> To bow and to bend
> We will not be ashamed.

(Drop arms, make a full body turnaround, and sing:)

> To turn, to turn
> Will be our delight.
> And turning, turning
> We'll come around right!

(Rejoin hands and repeat dance two more times.)

A Ritual for Croagh Patrick Pilgrimage (the last weekend of July) and Lughnassadh (the beginning of the harvest, August 1)

(In his poem "The Second Coming," William Butler Yeats wrote about a center that would not hold. This ritual is best celebrated outside on a hilltop.)

LEADER: We come to a high place as Saint Patrick did to Croagh Patrick Mountain—seeking a better vision. By our prayers and our actions, we will envision crops free from excessive pesticides, rivers clean again, and animals raised in natural settings. And so we pray:

ALL (or alternate verses):

O God, at the very center
From whom all being ripples forth,
Bring us to the circled Celtic cross.
There to be saved.
There to be healed.
There to be enlivened.

For without Jesus at the crux,
The center does not hold.
Without reverence all around,
The center does not hold.
Without recycling and reviving—
The great circle is broken—
The center does not hold.
The whales sing sad songs.
The bear, fewer woods to roam.

Rainforests, torched and trampled.
Rivers choked and clogged.
Mea culpa! Mea culpa!
Mea maxima culpa!

Ask the ancient Celts.
They shall tell you.
The trees do sing!
The rocks do speak!
The soil gives birth!
God's breath fills the earth!
We live on earth's circle.
Christ's halo–moon, sun, and stars.
To heal the circle is to recircle.
To heal is to forgive and to mend.
This day, let me heal my circle,
Blessing and reverencing all around.

LEADER: We walk in the holy circle, just as the Celts (and the Native Americans) prayed.

ALL:
(Arms extended forward)
    I walk with beauty before me.

(Arms extended down)
    I walk with beauty beneath me.

(Arms extended back)
    I walk with beauty behind me.

(Arms raised upward)
   I walk with beauty above me.

(Full body turning around)
   I walk with beauty all around me.

(Facing center)
   Your world is so beautiful, O God.

(Repeat twice.)

GLOSSARY

Adonai: traditional Jewish for Yahweh (God), to avoid the use of "Lord," which has sexist and classist connotations

affirmation: a visualization of a desired result and affirming to oneself that it is indeed happening; closely related to the ancient custom of blessing oneself "In the Name of the Father and of the Son and of the Holy Spirit," which affirms and reinforces identification with the holy Trinity

air: tune or melody

anam cara (Gaelic): "soul friend," a sharer of intimate soul concerns

Angelus: midday prayers when church bells ring; contains Hail Marys and angelic salutations

Anne, Saint: mother of Mary, replaced the ancient mother goddess, Anna, especially in Brittany

Antrim: an area in the north of Ireland renowned for its beautiful glens

Armagh: the primary bishop's see in Ireland

Bantry Bay: an ocean bay in the west of Cork

Beltane Blessing: a custom of the ancient Celts observed on May 1 when a ceremonial community fire was lit and people and animals passed through a divide in the fire for purification and protection

Bobbio: site near the Bobbio River in northern Italy where Saint Columbanus established a monastic site in the sixth century

Breastplate: the "shapeshifting" prayer Saint Patrick and his companions used on a dangerous journey

Brendan, Saint, "the Navigator": sixth century; the medieval epic, Navagatio Sancti Brendani, would seem to indicate that the explorer, Brendan, accompanied by other monks, reached the New World in the sixth century

Brigid, Saint, also called Bride and Brigit: sixth century; with Saint Patrick, most revered of Celtic saints. She was a warm and high-spirited woman revered by both men and women. Her double monastery, of men and women, was a sixth century innovation. Brigid took sexual equality as a given. As an abbess, she recruited a bishop as a helper. Her feast day, February 1, corresponds to the pagan cult of light and fire. In Celtic lore, the saint took on many of the attributes of a sun and fire deity. Saint Brigid was revered as caretaker of family, hearth, childbearing, and abundant harvest. Her feast marked the emergence from winter. Supplanting the pagan goddess, she harnessed the fire of the sun and delivered it to the hearth. Her cross of reeds is often seen over hearths in Ireland.

Brigid's shrine: at Kildare, where nuns kept an eternal flame burning for hundreds of years until it was extinguished by the invader Cromwell; also refers to many sacred wells in her honor throughout Ireland

Carmina Gadelica: a collection of oral hymns and incantations compiled in book form in the last century by

Alexander Carmichael, from the highlands and islands of Scotland. Some prayers are subtitled, referring to their origins.

Cavan: a northern county in the republic of Ireland

céad míle fáilte (Gaelic): "100,000 welcomes!"

Celtic spirituality: denotes special characteristics of prayer, devotion, and worldview that come down to us from a golden age, approximately 500-700 A.D., when Ireland became known as the land of "saints and scholars." (It has roots in pre-Christian Celtic experience. This special "Celtic flavor" of Christianity did not emerge from the womb of the Roman empire. Instead, Patrick and other missionaries took what was compatible in pagan usage and planted the seeds of the gospel in this rich soil.)

Celts: originally appearing in western Europe about 500 B.C.E., when they crossed the Rhine and moved westward, eventually as far as Scotland and Ireland; identifiable Celtic cultural traits found today in Brittany, Wales, and especially Scotland and Ireland

Clare, Saint of Assisi: thirteenth-century friend of Saint Francis and foundress of the Poor Clares

Clydesdale: a huge draft horse bred in Scotland

Colm Cille (Gaelic), Columba (Latin), Saint: the "dove"; the man who loved books; sixth century; one of the major patrons of Ireland. Not always a dove, he fought a battle at the foot of Ben Bulben's Head in County Sligo over a copy of the Psalter. He also went on trial over his claim to a book he illuminated. The Irish claim that copyright laws originated with this trial. Horrified at the deaths he caused, he exiled himself to Scotland and founded the crown jewel of monastic foundations on the island of Iona. He became active there in the conversion of the Pictish Scots. He later returned to Ireland to defend poets threatened with exile. The whole Celtic poetic tradition owes its survival to Colm Cille.

Columbanus, Saint: sixth century; wandered from Ireland founding monastic settlements which were islands of learning in a dark age. His monks successfully tilled the land. He established foundations at locales in today's France, Switzerland, Germany, and finally on the banks of the Bobbio River in northern Italy. A brilliant abbot, austere in his spirituality, he found solace and comfort when he went into the forests and communicated with the animals and birds–a trait found often in the Celts. The revered memory of Columbanus lived on at Bobbio and may have influenced Saint Francis or even Hildegard in the Rhineland.

Connemara: a breed of Irish ponies bred in the Connemara area in Galway

Constance, Countess Markievicz: Anglo-Irish patriot, one of the leaders of the 1916 Easter Rising, condemned to death but finally reprieved, married to the Polish Count Markievicz

Croagh Patrick: mountain peak in County Mayo, Ireland, where Patrick fasted and prayed during a Lenten season on his way to the conversion of Ireland; a pilgrimage site since Patrick's time in the fifth century, and before that a sacred mountain for the Druids. A memorial to the nineteenth century famine victims is located at its foot.

crofter: one who rents and cultivates a croft or small holding in the highlands and islands of Scotland; also one who bleaches linen on the grass

Cuchulainn: epic mythic hero of Ulster

David, Saint: sixth century; patron of Wales, preached respect and reverence in relationships

dualistic: viewing the world as divided by contrasting opposites. (For example, sometimes in Western world history, body was seen as bad and soul as good. This way of thinking was foreign to the Celts who saw all reality flowing together and divinity present everywhere.)

Dun Laoghaire: a ferry-docking suburb of Dublin

Edinburgh: major city in Scotland, site of Edinburgh Castle containing the chapel of Saint Margaret

Erin: a derivative of Eire, the name of Ireland

fairies: wee creatures who safeguard nature, thought to be either survivors of an old Irish tribe or fallen angels deserving of neither heaven nor hell. Some fairies are identified as remnants of a former people who went underground after the Celts invaded; others are identified as the gods of the earth. Some fairies troop together; others are solitary.

famine: in Ireland, a series of famine years in the 1840s, which cut the population in half as a result of deaths and emigrations

fosterling: a foster child. (A Celtic legend had Brigid as a midwife for the fosterling Christ Child. In Irish practice, it was not uncommon to place children with others for several years to help with their raising.)

Francis, Saint of Assisi: thirteenth century; creation-centered mystic, lover of birds and animals; experienced a kinship with all creation, including Brother Sun and Sister Moon. (In his book, *Saint Francis: Nature Mystic,* author Edward Armstrong suggests a Celtic influence upon Saint Francis, in particular from Saint Columbanus who, centuries before, settled in Bobbio in northern Italy.)

Gaels: Gaelic-speaking Celts

Gairloch: village at the head of Gair Loch, an inlet of the Atlantic Ocean on the northwest coast of Scotland

Georgian doors: colorful doors found on town houses in Dublin

Giants' Causeway: identical symmetrical rock formations on the northeast coast of Ireland

Glendalough: sixth-century monastic foundations containing Saint Kevin's Oratory in County Wicklow

gorse: a shrub with yellow blossoms, sometimes called "furze" in Ireland

hedgerow: a row of shrubs

Hilda, Saint: seventh century; renowned abbess who ruled a joint monastery of men and women at Whitby, advisor to laity and royalty. She took the side of the Celts at the Council of Whitby in their dispute with the Roman dating of Easter.

hillock: a small hill

Hildegard, abbess of Bingen: eleventh-century Benedictine in the Rhineland; a creation-centered mystic, artist, musician, composer. Her Celtic roots go back to when the Celts emerged in central Europe.

holy circle: pre-Christian people worldwide reverenced and prayed in the circle. Today, pilgrims at the shrines of Saint Brigid and atop Croagh Patrick can be observed saying their prayers as they move about in a circle. A footnote of history: In 1845, during the Irish famine, the Native American Choctaw tribe suffered their "Trail of Tears" as they were evicted from their homeland. They commiserated with the starving Irish and gathered from their meager funds $712 to send to Ireland for famine relief. In the 1990s the Irish commemorated their ancestors' nineteenth-century starvation walk across the Mayo Mountains in which 600 people died. Because of their ancestors' historical connection to the Choctaw nation in the holy circle, Choctaw Chief Roberts was invited to Ireland to lead the commemorative walk. (Vincent Brown, Native American researcher, writes that the spirituality of the Native Americans most resembles that of the ancient Celts.)

Imbolc: pagan feast celebrated in February, as the first seeds stir in the ground. (Christian Celts replaced this feast with Saint Brigid's Day and also Candlemas, honoring Mary.)

Innisfree: an island in a lake in Sligo, Ireland, made famous by poet William Butler Yeats, who wrote that peace would drop down slowly at this enchanting lake

Iona: island near Scotland, where Saint Colm Cille established the crown jewel of Celtic monasteries in the sixth century, famous for beautifully handcrafted psalters

Ita, Saint of Limerick: sixth century; famous abbess who served as foster parent for Saint Brendan in his early childhood

Joachim, Saint: father of Mary, grandfather of Jesus

keen(ing): an orchestrated mourning wail done by some women at Irish wakes

Kevin, Saint of Glendalough: seventh century; lover of animals and birds. It is said a badger used to bring him a salmon to eat. His monastic settlement was between two lakes at Glendalough in the Wicklow Mountains.

Kildare: town in County Kildare, the site of Saint Brigid's monastic foundation

kine: cattle

Knock: a popular pilgrimage site in County Mayo where visions occurred in the nineteenth century

legal tender: money. In Ireland, the five-pound note was sometimes affectionately called "the mercy note."

leprechaun: shoemaker fairy who works constantly and keeps his money in a pot at the end of the rainbow

Lisdoonvarna: town in County Clare, Ireland, where a fall festival still draws bachelors who sometimes seek a match through the good offices of a marriage broker

Liturgy of the Hours: see "Psalter"

loch: lake

Lourdes: famous healing shrine in the Pyrenees Mountains in southern France

Lughnassadh: a pagan festival celebrated in August, marking the start of the harvest

Macha: the gray mare of the epic hero, Cuchulainn. Foreseeing the hero's death, the horse wept tears of blood.

Maeve: Celtic Queen of Connacht, mythologized as the strong Celtic woman whose power and daring could exceed that of powerful men

Margaret, Saint of Scotland: eleventh century; a pious queen, friend of the poor whose chapel is contained in the castle overlooking Edinburgh

marriage brokers: after the harvest in Lisdoonvarna, County Clare, bachelors and maidens, young and old, flock to the fair and, as in days past and still today, marriage brokers can be seen moving about arranging matches

McAuley, Sister Catherine: nineteenth-century foundress of the Sisters of Mercy in Dublin

Mochaoi, Saint: seventh-century Irish monk enchanted by a bird, perhaps a shapeshifted angel

Newgrange: a large rock-encased mound over 4000 years old in the northeast of the Republic of Ireland, featuring a narrow corridor that runs to its center. At the time of the winter solstice, a beam of light from the sun moves up the corridor like a sword and illumines inscribed rocks at the center.

Non, Saint: sixth century; mother of Saint David, name derived from the name of the pagan mother goddess

o' lang syne: (auld lang syne): "Old long then," referring to former good old days and friends

O'Malley, Grace: sixteenth century; swashbuckling pirate who conquered by heroics and charm her castle on Clare Island. What she could not win by sword, she charmed from Queen Elizabeth.

original blessing: the beautiful, evolutionary unfolding of creation for millions of years before humans came into being on the planet. (The ancient Celts believed that the creatures who were on the planet long before humans had a wisdom that could instruct humans.)

original sin: a relatively recent human eruption of evil which occurred only after millions of years of evolutionary development

pagan: from the Latin *paganus,* meaning "a country person"

paps: two hills in Kerry attributed to be the breasts of the divine mother, Danu or Anu

Pangor Ban: cat mentioned in famous Celtic monk's poem

Patrick, Saint: fifth century; patron of Ireland; kidnapped from his homeland and spent part of his youth enslaved in Ireland. After escaping back to his home, he heard the voices of the Irish in a dream calling him back. His was the first voice in Western civilization to condemn slavery.

Patrick's Purgatory: an Island on Lough Derge, a pilgrimage site where Saint Patrick did penance; still a special place of penitential pilgrimage for the Irish

Plunkett, Joseph Mary: poet ("I See His Blood Upon the Rose"); one of the leaders in the 1916 Easter Rising

pioneers: Irish temperance society members

Psalter: book of psalms and readings containing the Liturgy of the Hours which set off eight prayer times throughout the day, including Matins, Lauds, Prime, Terce, Sext, Nones, Vespers, and Compline.

reeks: mountains

Salmon of Knowledge: a mythological salmon in the River Boyne which possessed deep knowledge and wisdom. The first person to catch and eat it would know all there was to know.

sevenfold blessing: Celtic folklore believed that sometimes the seventh son of a seventh son possessed special
powers of healing, as did holy wells and the intercessions
of Saint Brigid and Saint Patrick.

shapeshift(ed): the ancient Celtic belief that humans can
transform themselves into animal appearances. (A legend
has Saint Patrick "shapeshifting" into a deer on one
occasion to avoid his enemies.)

sheiling: from the root word meaning to hunt or to chase;
also a mountain pasture. "Sheiling time" was a gay time of
full summer pastures, blooming heather, and lads and
maidens dancing.

Siloam's holy pool: a pool where Jesus healed (John 9:7)

Skellig Michael: a rocky redoubt eight miles off the coast
of Kerry that juts up 600 feet out of the wild Atlantic.
Ancient monastic beehive cells remain, evidence that
humans lived and prayed here, cut off from the mainland,
having to make it on their own. On its brow—a solitary
lighthouse.

Talbot, Matt: nineteenth-century patron of the Irish
temperance movement

Three: ancient Celtic mystical number, three goddesses,
three realms, three-leaf shamrock, and finally the holy
Trinity

white martyrdom: holy practices of difficult fasts, long
journeys, and exiles, as there were no blood martyrs
during the conversion of Ireland

ABOUT THIS BOOK

A Contemporary Celtic Prayer Book is a unique and beautiful prayer book that captures the flavor and sensibility of traditional Celtic spirituality for today's Christians.

Part One of this book contains a simplified Liturgy of the Hours that presents morning, midday and evening prayers for a seven-day period. Additional prayers and variations allow this cycle of prayers to be used week after week.

Part Two offers a treasury of Celtic blessings, prayers and rituals for a variety of ordinary and special occasions.

"Readers will be charmed and inspired! Father Fitzgerald's practical guide to prayer and meditation for today's pilgrims blends Celtic mystery and poetry with the author's own creative Irish experience."

Bob Reilly
Author, Irish Saints

"Instead of reading about Celtic spirituality of yore, we're invited to taste it today—and it is good."

Dolores Curran
Author and Syndicated Columnist

ABOUT THE AUTHOR

WILLIAM JOHN FITZGERALD, a Catholic priest, writes from his rich experience of nearly forty years as a parish priest in the Archdiocese of Omaha. He is the author of many books including *Beyond Easter, Seasons of the Earth and Heart, 100 Cranes* and *Stories of Coming Home.* He resides at Our Lady of Perpetual Help Parish in Scottsdale, Arizona, where he is officially retired but continues to write, present adult workshops and minister in the parish.